THE DEATH RITUALS OF RURAL GREECE

THE
DEATH RITUALS
OF RURAL
GREECE

BY

LORING M. DANFORTH

PHOTOGRAPHY BY

ALEXANDER TSIARAS

PRINCETON UNIVERSITY PRESS
PRINCETON, NEW JERSEY

Copyright © 1982 by Princeton University Press

Published by Princeton University Press, 41 William Street,
Princeton, New Jersey 08540

In the United Kingdom: Princeton University Press,
Chichester, West Sussex

All Rights Reserved

Library of Congress Cataloging in Publication Data will be
found on the last printed page of this book

Princeton University Press books are printed on acid-free paper
and meet the guidelines for permanence and durability of the
Committee on Production Guidelines for Book Longevity
of the Council on Library Resources

Printed in the United States of America by Princeton Academic Press

DESIGNED BY LAURY A. EGAN

6 7 8 9 10

iv

CONTENTS

v

PREFACE

THIS BOOK had its genesis in a trip Alexander Tsiaras made to the village in northern Greece his parents had left some thirty-five years earlier. He lived there from June 1975 to June 1976, coming to know his relatives and photographing many aspects of rural Greek life. He was particularly impressed with the powerful drama of the rituals surrounding death and realized that they would be an interesting and unusual topic for a photographic essay. After returning to the United States, he showed his photographs of funerals, memorial services, and exhumations to Gail Filion at Princeton University Press, who encouraged him to approach an anthropologist about the possibility of writing an analysis of these rituals, which, together with the photographs, would comprise a valuable contribution to the study of the ritual and religious life of rural Greece. In the spring of 1979 Alexander Tsiaras invited me to join him in this project, and I accepted enthusiastically. That summer, in the same village where Alexander Tsiaras had lived several years earlier, I carried out the fieldwork on which this study is based. Given the history of this book, it should be clear that the photographs presented here are not intended simply as illustrations of the text. Rather they constitute an independently conceived visual commentary on the death rituals of rural Greece, one which complements, in the best sense of the word, the anthropological analysis it accompanies.

Many people have made important contributions to this project. Alexander Tsiaras would like to thank his parents, Mr. and Mrs. George Tsiaras, as well as Milton and Christos Tsiaras for providing him with financial and moral support. Mr. W. Heun and Mrs. R. Greico of E. Leitz, Inc., generously furnished photographic equipment for this project, while Mr. Curtis Roseman ensured the quality and the integrity of the printing of the photographs. The assistance of Olympic Airways is also gratefully acknowledged.

I would like to thank the following people who have been kind enough to read an earlier draft of this book and offer very helpful and much appreciated criticisms and suggestions: Margaret Alexiou, Vincent Crapanzano, Jill Dubisch, Dimitri Gondicas, Michael Herzfeld, Steven Kemper, Gail Kligman, and Roy Wagner. I would like to express my sincerest gratitude to Gail Filion of Princeton University Press, whose enthusiasm for this project has been a constant source of encouragement. I would also like to thank William Hively for his editorial assistance, Lillian Morency for typing the various drafts of this book, and the reference librarians of the Bates College Library. My parents taught me the value and the joy of learning, and my wife, Margaret Rotundo, helped me immeasurably during the writing of this book with her patience and her good advice. I thank them as well.

Many people in Greece offered me their warm friendship and their generous hospitality. The eagerness with which they shared their lives, their language, and their culture with me made it a joy to live and work in Greece. In particular I would like to thank Xenophon and Sophia Tenezakis and Yannis and Olga Lappas.

Finally, both Alexander Tsiaras and I would like to thank Glykeria Karayiorgou, who took us both into her home and cared for us well. More importantly, she was genuinely curious about her own culture and relished the challenge of making sense of her world in a new way. She participated eagerly in the anthropological endeavor. Without her this book would not have been possible.

LORING M. DANFORTH
Lewiston, Maine
August 1981

THE DEATH RITUALS OF RURAL GREECE

Τὰ τραγούδια λόγια εἶναι, τὰ λέν' οἱ πικραμένοι.
Τὰ λέν' νὰ βγάλουν τὸ πικρό, μὰ τὸ πικρὸ δὲ βγαίνει.

Songs are just words. Those who are bitter sing them.
They sing them to get rid of their bitterness, but the
      bitterness doesn't go away.

INTRODUCTION:

THE SELF AND THE OTHER

ANTHROPOLOGY inevitably involves an encounter with the Other. All too often, however, the ethnographic distance that separates the reader of anthropological texts and the anthropologist himself from the Other is rigidly maintained and at times even artificially exaggerated. In many cases this distancing leads to an exclusive focus on the Other as primitive, bizarre, and exotic. The gap between a familiar "we" and an exotic "they" is a major obstacle to a meaningful under-standing of the Other, an obstacle that can only be overcome through some form of participation in the world of the Other.

The maintenance of this ethnographic distance has resulted in what Johannes

Fabian (1973) has called the parochialization or the folklorization of the anthropological inquiry into death. Rather than confronting the universal significance of death, anthropologists have often trivialized death by concerning themselves with the exotic, curious, and at times violent ritual practices that accompany death in many societies. As a consequence "anthropological studies of death have been, by and large, assigned the role of providing the exotic 'other' to the sociologist's 'we' " (Fabian 1973:187). If, however, it is possible to reduce the distance between the anthropologist and the Other, to bridge the gap between "us" and "them," then the goal of a truly humanistic anthropology can be achieved. This achievement involves the full realization that both "we" and "they" share a common humanity. As Claude Lévi-Strauss has said: "When an exotic custom fascinates us in spite of (or on account of) its apparent singularity, it is generally because it presents us with a distorted reflection of a familiar image, which we confusedly recognize as such without yet managing to identify it" (1966a:238–239).

Any serious inquiry into another culture, therefore, leads to a greater understanding of one's own culture. An investigation of the Other involves an exploration of the Self as well. The central problem of anthropology is thus, in Paul Ricoeur's words, "the comprehension of the self by the detour of the comprehension of the other" (Rabinow 1977:5). The anthropologist sets out to investigate the Other, only to find the Other in himself and himself in the Other. For the anthropology of death, this means that the study of "how others die" becomes the study of "how we die" (Fabian 1973). We must come to see in the deaths of Others our own deaths as well.

Johannes Fabian suggests a theoretical perspective that would enable an anthropologist interested in death to transcend a parochial concern for exotic rites. It is this theoretical perspective that I have adopted in the present study of death rituals in rural Greece. With Fabian, I see the human experience of death as the core of a universal language or code. Through the rituals and symbols that constitute this language people cope with the threat of death. The performance of death-related rituals is an attempt to mediate the opposition between life and death by asserting that death is an integral part of life. Death, in fact, provides an opportunity to affirm the continuity and meaning of life itself.

The desire to collapse the distance between Self and Other which prompted the adoption of this theoretical stance springs from my fieldwork. Whenever I observed death rituals in rural Greece, I was acutely aware of a paradoxical sense of simultaneous distance and closeness, otherness and oneness. On one hand, the notebook and the tape recorder I held in my hands separated me from the bereaved women around me. To my eyes funeral laments, black mourning dress, and exhumation rites *were* exotic. Yet on the other hand, I was conscious at all times that it is not just Others who die. I was aware that my friends and relatives will die, that I will die, that death comes to all, Self and Other alike.

Over the course of my fieldwork these "exotic" rites became meaningful, even attractive alternatives to the experience of death as I had known it. As I sat by the body of a man who had died several hours earlier and listened to his wife, his sisters, and his daughters lament his death, I imagined these rites being performed and these laments being sung at the death of my relatives, at my own death. It was a comforting thought. It made sense. When the brother of the deceased entered the room, the women gathered there began to sing a lament about two brothers who were violently separated as they sat clinging to each other in the branches of a tree that was being swept away by a raging torrent. I thought of my own brother and cried. The distance between Self and Other had grown small indeed.

This book is an attempt to communicate both an intellectual and an emotional response to the death rituals of rural Greece. Its format is designed to minimize the distance between the reader and the Greek villagers whose lives and deaths are presented here; to enable the reader to come to see these rites not as something distant and exotic but rather, in the words of Lévi-Strauss, as "a distorted reflection of a familiar image." The narrative account in Chapter 1 and the photographic essay are intended to provide the reader with a vivid image of the people, the Others, whose lives and deaths are given meaning through the performance of these rituals. In addition, the texts of the many funeral laments presented here should be read as evocative and poetic statements of the bereaved women of rural Greece which attest directly to the richness and power of their response to death.

I hope that this form of presentation will enable the reader to transcend, at least in part, the opposition between Self and Other, to see himself in the Others presented here, and to see his death in the deaths of the people of rural Greece. It will then be apparent that this book is not just about how Others die, but about how we die as well.

1

DEATH IN POTAMIA

THE VILLAGE OF POTAMIA lies at the edge of a small plain in northern Thessaly, twenty-five miles to the southwest of Mount Olympus. It occupies a triangle of flat land, bounded on two sides by the wide, rocky beds of the Titarisios and one of its tributaries. On the third side rise low hills, rounded, gray, and barren except for outcroppings of scrub oak, which provide meager pasturage for the sheep and goats of the area. In sharp contrast to these stone-covered slopes, fertile land stretches off below the town into the haze of the foothills in the distance. Here lie small rectangular fields of bright green tobacco, yellow wheat, and red, freshly plowed earth. Between the fields stand rows of poplar trees, living fences that mature and grow until they are cut for fuel in the winter.

Irrigation and increased mechanization have brought prosperity to the six hundred inhabitants of Potamia. Their well built two-story houses and barns are surrounded by gray cinder block walls, which divide the town into family court-yards. The one structure that rises above the red brick roof tiles of the village is the bell tower of the church, a nesting site for the storks that return from Africa every spring. Beside the church, near the juncture of the two dry riverbeds, lies the village graveyard. It was here I had come on a hot, cloudless afternoon in July 1979 to learn how the people of rural Greece deal with death.

Upon entering the graveyard of Potamia through an old wooden gate, I was immediately struck by how small it was. Twenty-one graves, set very close together, extended in three rows from the gate to a mass of tangled vines and bushes on the far side. The graves fell into two distinct categories. A few were marked off by a rectangular fence of metal or wood, a cage-like enclosure around bare earth or gravel (Plate 13). At the head of each grave, attached to the grillwork, was a box, sometimes shaped like a house with a peaked roof and a chimney, on top of which stood a cross. Here were kept a photograph of the deceased, an oil lamp, and matches and wicks with which to light it (Plate 16).

Most of the graves were much more elaborate and expensive. White marble slabs, set in cement, formed a raised platform in the center of which was an area covered with gravel, where flowering plants grew. At the head of these graves were marble plaques bearing the name and the dates of birth and death of the deceased. Above the plaques rose marble crosses often decorated with wreaths of plastic flowers. To the right and left of each headstone stood a small box with glass sides and a marble top. One box contained a framed photograph; the other, an oil lamp, a bottle of olive oil, and a jar of dried flower blossoms used as wicks. At the foot of each grave was a large metal container half filled with sand, in which stood the stubs of candles extinguished by the wind (Plates 18 and 20).

As I walked between two rows of graves, I noticed that no grave bore a date of death prior to 1974. The explanation for this, and for the small size of the graveyard as well, lay in a small cement building standing in the corner of the graveyard (Plates 16 and 31). Although I knew what I would find inside, I was still not fully prepared for the sight that confronted me when I opened the door.

Beyond a small floor-space a ladder led down to a dark, musty-smelling area filled with the bones of many generations of villagers. Near the top of the huge pile the remains of each person were bound up separately in a white cloth. Toward the bottom of the pile the bones—skulls, pelvises, ribs, the long bones of countless arms and legs—lay in tangled disarray, having lost all trace of belonging to distinct individuals with the disintegration of the cloth wrappings. Stacked in one corner of the building were metal boxes and small suitcases with names, dates, and photographs identifying the people whose bones lay securely within.

At the sound of the church bell calling the village women to vespers, I went out into the bright sunlight. A few minutes later a woman entered the graveyard, dressed entirely in black, with a black kerchief covering her forehead, hair, and neck (Plate 17). She carried one large white candle and a handful of small yellow ones. After crossing herself three times she lit the white candle and one yellow one at the grave of the person she had come to mourn. Then she went up and down the rows of graves placing candles in the sand-filled containers at the foot of several other graves. Finally she returned to the first grave and began the elaborate procedure of preparing and lighting the oil lamp by the headstone.

Soon the graveyard was alive with activity, and a forest of candles burned at the foot of each grave. About ten women, all dressed in shades of black, brown, or blue, busied themselves lighting lamps and sweeping around the graves. Several women began hauling water in large buckets from the faucet in the church courtyard nearby. After watering the flowers on the graves they were caring for, the women began to wash the marble headstones with sponges and detergent kept in little plastic bags hidden carefully in the grass by the graveyard wall. So attentive was their care for the graves that some women would sift through the sand-filled containers throwing out clumps of melted wax or scrape old wax off the marble slabs with small knives kept just for that purpose.

After fifteen or twenty minutes, when most of this housecleaning had been completed, the atmosphere in the graveyard once again turned somber and quiet. Each woman sat on the grave of her husband, parent, or child, tending the candles and talking quietly with women at nearby graves. They discussed their crops, the weather, or the long-awaited summer visits of their children working far away in Athens, Germany, and the United States. Often their conversations dealt with matters closer at hand—funerals in neighboring villages, the expense of renting a cemetery plot in a large city, or the circumstances surrounding the deaths of their relatives who lay buried beneath them.

One woman sat near the head of a grave, staring at a photograph of a young woman. She rocked gently back and forth, sobbing and crying. Suddenly she began to sing a lament in a pained, almost angry tone of voice. Before she finished the long, melismatic line of the first verse she was joined by other women. The intensity of emotion in the women's voices quickly increased. The verses of the lament, sung in unison by the chorus of mourners, alternated with breaks during which each woman shouted a personal message addressed to her own dead relative.

"Ah! Ah! Ah! My unlucky Eleni."

"Nikos, what pain you have caused us. You poisoned our hearts."

"Kostas, my Kostas, the earth has eaten your beauty and your youth."

These cries were interrupted by the next verse, as the singing resumed. When the first lament ended, a woman sitting in the far corner of the graveyard immediately began a second. Finally, after singing three or four laments lasting perhaps fifteen minutes in all, the women stopped. The loud songs and cries were followed by quiet sobbing and hushed conversations.

Several women stood up, crossed themselves, and announced that it was time to leave. They tried to comfort the women who had shouted the loudest, whose grief seemed to be the most intense, by telling them to have patience, to be strong, and to remember that they accomplished nothing by carrying on so. Two or three of the most grief-stricken women said that they would stay a few more minutes, until the candles burned out; but the other women continued to urge them to leave, saying: "In the end we'll all come here. Even if we sit here all night, the dead still won't return from the grave." After several such exchanges all the women agreed to leave. About an hour after their arrival, they filed out of the graveyard one by one and returned slowly to their homes, to the world of the living.

This sequence of events was repeated daily with only slight variation during my stay in Potamia. I spent my first few evenings at the graveyard standing awkwardly in the corner by the gate, feeling extremely out of place. Several days later my situation became less uncomfortable when Irini, the woman who had begun the lament my first evening in the graveyard, gestured toward the grave on her right and suggested I sit down. That was the beginning of the process by which I came to know these women and to understand the manner in which they experienced death.

The death of Irini's twenty-year-old daughter Eleni was generally acknowledged to have been the most tragic the village of Potamia had experienced in many years. Eleni died almost five years earlier, in August 1974. She had been a very attractive young woman, tall, with long black hair. Since she had been one of the best students in the village elementary school, her parents decided to send her to high school in the city of Elassona, about ten miles away. This involved tremendous sacrifice for her and her family, since at that time there was no regular means of transportation between Potamia and Elassona. As a result, from the age of twelve Eleni lived alone, away from her village, her home, and her family. Several times a week her father would walk to Elassona to bring her food. Since she had done well in high school, Eleni went on to study for two more years in order to become an elementary-school teacher.

One month before she was to begin her first teaching job, Eleni was struck by a car and killed in a hit-and-run accident in the city of Thessaloniki. Several of Eleni's relatives who lived in Thessaloniki were notified of her death by the police. They put on brightly colored clothes and came immediately by taxi to Potamia, having packed black clothes of mourning in their suitcases. When Irini saw them approaching her house, she asked why they had come. They told her that they brought good news and asked her to call her husband and her children, who were working in the fields. When the entire family had gathered, the visitors told them they in fact were bringing bad news: Eleni had been killed. They then changed into their black clothes, placed a photograph of Eleni on the floor in the center of the room, and began the funeral vigil amid wild cries and laments.

The arrival of the body was delayed until the following day because an autopsy had to be performed. When the body finally arrived in Potamia, neighbors and more distant relatives advised burying it right away, but Irini would have no part of it. She wanted her daughter to spend her last night in her family home, which she had been away from for so many years. After a second all-night vigil, Eleni was buried wearing in death the white bridal dress and wedding crown she had been unable to wear in life.

For a full year after her daughter's death, Irini stayed inside her house. She did not want to see people; she did not want to see the light of day. For a full year she did not even go to church, nor did she visit her mother who lived on the other side of the village. The only reason she left her house was to come to

13

the graveyard to be with her daughter. She would come late at night and in mid-afternoon when other people were sleeping, so that she would not see anyone. Often her husband or her children would come to the graveyard to take her home, but she would return as soon as they left her alone. Eleni's father would also come to his daughter's grave and lament like a woman. He would even sing laments while he was herding his sheep and goats in the hills above the village. People working in the fields heard him and cried.

For the next five years Irini wore black. She never had a chance to put on the red shoes she had bought the week before Eleni's death. Every day without fail for five years she came to her daughter's grave, once in the morning and then again in the evening. She attended all the funerals and memorial services in Potamia and the surrounding villages so she could lament, cry, and express the pain she felt. She knew full well, though, that the wound of a mother never heals, that her pain never ceases. Several years after Eleni's death, Irini's other daughter was married. Irini did not attend the wedding herself, and she refused to allow any singing or dancing in her house on the wedding day. Now, whenever her son-in-law, who lives with Irini and her husband, listens to music on the radio, Irini becomes upset. She says that her heart is poisoned.

Since her daughter's death Irini has become very close to another village woman, Maria. They say they are neighbors in a way, because Maria's son Kostas is buried in the grave next to Eleni. The two bereaved mothers have spent many hours together sitting on their children's graves and sharing each other's pain. Kostas died at age thirty in 1975, just one year after Eleni. He had lived with his wife and young son for several years in Germany, where he worked in a factory. However, because his marriage was unsuccessful, he returned to Greece and found a job as a construction worker in a nearby city. Since his wife, who remained in Germany to continue working, was unable to care for her son, Kostas brought him to Potamia to live with Maria and her husband. Several months later Kostas was killed when the cement frame of the apartment building where he was working collapsed and crushed him. Maria, who blames her daughter-in-law for having made the last few years of her son's life unhappy, is quick to mention that her daughter-in-law did not return from Germany for Kostas' funeral. When she finally did come to the village a year later to visit her son, she was not even dressed in black.

14

During the many evenings I sat in the graveyard near Maria and Irini I learned much about their encounters with death. Maria would tell Irini how, when no one else is in the house, she takes out some of her son's clothes and hugs them and cries and sings laments. Irini would discuss the dreams that she and her husband had seen prior to Eleni's accident. They now realized that these dreams had clearly foretold their daughter's death. One night Irini had seen her daughter, dressed as a bride, leaving home in a taxi. As all the dream books say, dreams of weddings are ominous signs of impending death. A week before Eleni's death, her father had seen in his sleep a herd of black goats descending the hill toward his pens at the edge of the village.

By mid-July these conversations turned increasingly to the events that would soon cause Maria and Irini renewed grief and pain. At the end of the month Eleni would be exhumed. According to custom this had to be done before she had completed five full years in the ground. She would be exhumed because her family wanted to see her for the last time and because she should not have to bear the weight of the earth on her chest for eternity. She would be exhumed so that she could see once more the light of the sun. During the weeks before the exhumation Irini sang laments more frequently and cried out to her daughter more emotionally:

Eleni, Eleni, you died far from home with no one near you. I've shouted and cried for five years, Eleni, my unlucky one, but you haven't heard me. I don't have the courage to shout any more. Eleni, Eleni, my lost soul. You were a young plant, but they didn't let you blossom. You've been here for five years. Soon you'll leave. Then where will I go? What will I do? Five years ago I put a beautiful bird into the ground, a beautiful partridge. But now what will I take out? Now what will I find?

At other times Irini calmly and sadly made plans to dismantle her daughter's grave. She gave most of the flowers she had watered faithfully for five years to Maria to place on Kostas' grave. She gave the sand-filled metal container at the foot of Eleni's grave to the widow of a poor man who had recently died. The marble monument itself would be reused for the grave of the next villager to die. What had been for the past five years a home for both Irini and her daughter would soon be destroyed.

15

One evening Maria arrived at the graveyard very troubled and upset. As soon as she sat down on her son's grave, she began to cry and sob uncontrollably. When she had regained her composure slightly, she told Irini that she had just received a letter from her daughter-in-law saying that she had decided to take her son away from Potamia and bring him to live with her in Germany. At the end of the month, on the very day Eleni was to be exhumed, Maria's grandson would be taken away from her. Maria told Irini that her grandson had been her only source of joy since her son's death. While the boy was with her, she said, it was as if her son Kostas were still alive. Her grandson's departure would be as painful for her as her son's death. It would be like a second funeral.

The evening before the exhumation of Eleni and the departure of Maria's grandson for Germany, the young boy, no more than seven years old, accompanied his grandmother to his father's grave. He was eating candy and seemed in his innocence completely unaware of the emotional power the situation held for his grandmother and others. At Maria's insistence he lit a candle and placed it on his father's grave. Then he asked if he could water the flowers on the grave. He did so with difficulty, struggling under the weight of the large bucket of water. When he had finished, Maria took him in her arms and rocked him back and forth, overcome with tears. Gazing at her son's photograph, she began to sing:

1

Κάτω στὸν Ἄη Θόδωρο, στὸν Ἅγιο Κωσταντῖνο,
πανεγυρίτσι γίνονταν, μεγάλο πανεγύρι.
Τὸ πανεγύρ' ἦταν πολὺ κι ὁ τόπος ἦταν λίγος,
σαράντα δίπλες ὁ χορός, ἑξήντα δυὸ τραπέζια.
Τὸ ποιὸς τραβάει τὸ χορό, τὸ ποιὸς καὶ τὰ τραγούδια;
Ἑλένη σέρνει τὸ χορὸ κι ὁ Κώστας τὰ τραγούδια.
Κι ἀπ' τὸ πολύ της τὸ χορὸ κι ἀπ' τὰ πολλὰ τραγούδια,
γιόμισ' ὁ κάμπος κουρνιαχτὸς καὶ τὰ βουνὰ ἀντάρα.
Κι ἡ μάνα του τοὺς ἔλεγε κι ἡ μάνα του τοὺς λέει:
—Πάψτε, παιδιά μ', τὸ χορό, πάψτε καὶ τὰ τραγούδια,
νὰ κατακάτση ὁ κουρνιαχτός, νὰ σηκωθῆ ἡ ἀντάρα,
νὰ βροῦν οἱ μάνες τὰ παιδιὰ καὶ τὰ παιδιὰ τὶς μάνες,
νὰ βρῶ κι ἐγὼ τὸν Κώστα μου.

Down at the church of St. Theodore, down at the church of St.
    Constantine,
a festival was taking place, a huge festival.
The crowd was large, and there was little room.
There were forty rows of dancers and sixty-two tables.
Who is leading the dancing? Who is leading the singing?
Eleni is leading the dancing, and Kostas is leading the singing.
But from all the dancing and from all the singing
the plain filled with dust, and the mountains were covered with mist.
Then Kostas' mother said to them:
"My children, stop the dancing! Stop the singing!
So that the dust may settle, and the mist may rise,
so that mothers may find their children, and children may find their
    mothers,
and so that I may find Kostas, my son."

After this lament, Irini began another:

2

Ν' ἀκούσης καλά, μανούλα μου, τί θὰ σοῦ παραγγείλω.
Ὄντας σὲ πάρη ὁ πόνος σου κι ἡ φλόγ' ἀπ' τὴν καρδιά σου,
γιὰ κίνα κι ἔλα μιὰ βραδιὰ κι ἕνα Σαββάτο βράδυ,
καὶ κάτσε στὸ κεφάλι μου καὶ φώναξε: —Ἑλένη.
Κι ἂν δὲ σ' ἀκούσω μιὰ φορὰ κι ἂν δὲ σ' ἀκούσω πέντε,
κι ἀπὸ τοὺς πέντε καὶ μπροστὰ νὰ μὴν ξαναφωνάξης.
Φτιάσι τὰ νύχια σου τσαπὶ καὶ τὶς παλάμες φτυάρι.
Ρίξι τὸ χῶμα στὴ μεριὰ κι ἀνοίξι παραθύρι,
νὰ 'ρθῆς νὰ κουβεντιάσουμε, νὰ 'ρθῆς ν' ἀνταμωθοῦμε.
Ἂν εἶμαι ν-ἄσπρη κι ὅμορφη, σκύψι καὶ φίλησέ με.
Κι ἂν εἶμαι μαύρη κι ἄραχνη, ρίξι καὶ σκέπασέ με.
Σύρι, μάνα μ', στὸ σπίτι σου, σύρι καὶ στὰ παιδιά σου.
Φιάσι τὸ γιόμα ὅμορφο, τὸ δεῖπνο χαϊδεμένο.
Κι ἂν δὲ φανῶ στὸ γιόμα σου, κι ἂν δὲ φανῶ στὸ δεῖπνο,
ποτές, μάνα μ', μὴν καρτερῆς.

"Mother, listen well to what I ask of you.
When you are moved by the pain and the fire in your heart,
come down to the graveyard some evening, some Saturday evening,
and sit at my head and cry out: 'Eleni!'
If I don't hear you the first time, if I don't hear you the fifth time,
then don't cry out again.
Make your fingernails a hoe and your palms a shovel.
Throw the earth to the side and open a window,
so that you can come, and we can talk.
If I am white and beautiful, bend down and kiss me,
but if I am black and covered with cobwebs, cover me up again.
Mother, hurry home. Hurry home to your children.
Prepare a delicious lunch. Prepare a dinner with loving care.
If I don't appear at lunch, and if I don't appear at dinner,
then, mother, wait for me no longer."

Late the following afternoon women gathered at the house of Irini. There were relatives, close friends, and neighbors, many of them in mourning themselves for other dead, in other graves. They talked quietly about the good earth of Potamia and about the clean white bones of the village dead who had been exhumed in the past. Irini complained about how few relatives were present, adding that more people would have come if they were celebrating Eleni's wedding.

When the bell of the village church rang in a slow mournful rhythm, the group set out for the graveyard. Eleni's immediate family led the procession. Her father and her two brothers were the only men present. Behind them came more distant female relatives carrying offerings of food and drink to be distributed after the exhumation as well as the metal box that would receive Eleni's remains. With each house it passed the procession grew larger, as one or two women fell in behind the others.

Once inside the graveyard everyone closed tightly around Eleni's grave. Irini sat to one side of the headstone and immediately began to sing a lament. On her right sat her sister; on her left, Maria. Across the grave from Irini sat her husband; to his side Eleni's sisters and cousins. The remainder of the area immediately surrounding the grave was filled with other relatives and women in mourning. Behind them stood many more village women crowding in closely to follow the course of the exhumation (Plate 26). The clothes of all these women, numbering well over a hundred, formed concentric rings of color ranging outward from the circle of black in the center through a band of blues and browns to the bright colors worn by women who had not been so closely touched by death.

Eleni's two brothers, who had started to dig down through the gravel and sandy soil, were soon overcome with emotion, as the intensity of the lamenting increased. When they began to cry, two young women took their shovels and continued digging. Eleni's brothers withdrew to the outside of the circle of women, where they stood quietly and awkwardly, men out of place in a women's world of death.

The loud chorus of laments could not mask the sharp ring of the shovels against the earth, nor could it blot out the increasingly violent cries and shouts of Irini and Maria. As the gaping hole in the middle of the grave grew deeper, Irini leaned farther over the place where her daughter lay, until she had to be pulled back by her sister. Eleni's father, much more restrained in the expression of his grief, though no less intense, would occasionally cry out: "You didn't live to accomplish anything, Eleni, anything at all."

When the earth in the grave turned a much darker color, and fragments of rotten wood appeared, the singing grew louder. The young women with shovels were replaced in the grave by an older widow with a small hoe (Plate 28). Some women shouted instructions to her, telling her to dig carefully: "More to the right. Find the skull first, then the ribs. Don't break anything." When she struck something solid with her hoe, she put it down and began to dig with her hands. The singing grew weaker; the melody was carried now by only a few voices. Irini, Maria, and the other close relatives continued their wild, angry shouting.

When the widow uncovered the skull, she crossed herself and bent down to pick it up. People threw flowers into the grave. All singing stopped, while the screaming, shouting, and wailing reached a new peak. The widow tried to wipe what looked like hair off the back of the skull before she wrapped it in a white kerchief. She crossed herself again and placed some paper money on the skull outside the kerchief. Then she kissed the skull and handed it to Irini.

Irini cradled her daughter's skull in her arms, crying and sobbing uncon-

19

trollably. The women behind her tried to take it from her but she would not let go. She held Eleni's skull to her cheek, embracing it much as she would have embraced Eleni were she still alive. Finally she placed more paper money on the skull and wrapped another kerchief around it, a kerchief which had been embroidered by Eleni as part of her dowry. Irini kissed the skull and touched it to her forehead three times before she handed it to Maria, who did the same. Irini and Maria embraced the skull together for several minutes, shrieking and wailing. Then they handed it across the open grave to Eleni's father, who greeted his daughter's skull as the others had before him. It was then passed down the side of the grave to be greeted by sisters, brothers, cousins, and others.

As more bones were uncovered, they were placed in the metal box by the headstone. Irini took the photograph of Eleni, which had stood for five years in the glass case at the head of the grave, and placed it in the frame on the front of the box. Women tossed small coins into the box as it slowly filled with bones. Eleni's skull was returned to Irini, who held it in her lap for the remainder of the exhumation. Some women commented on the blackness of the bones and on how well preserved Eleni's shoes, stockings, and dress were. Others offered advice as to where to find the small bones of the hands and feet (Plate 27). Irini reached into the metal box and picked up a severed bone from one of Eleni's legs, which had apparently been broken when she was fatally injured. She dropped it back into the box, crying: "You were a beautiful young partridge, and they killed you."

The widow was still sifting through the earth, in search of a ring, a cross, and a gold tooth. The lamenting gradually ceased, and women began to exchange fatalistic comments about human mortality and the inevitability of death: "That's all we are, a pile of bones. We were born, and we will die. Then we'll all come here" (Plate 29). Two women counted the bones in the box and discussed the best way to arrange them. At last Irini was persuaded to let go of her daughter's skull and place it in the box on top of the other bones.

Suddenly all the women stood up and crossed themselves. The graveyard was filled with silence and the smell of incense. The village priest had arrived. He held a censer in one hand and a lit candle in the other. As everyone around the grave was handed a candle and lit it, the priest began to recite a portion of the Orthodox funeral service (Plate 21):

20

Everlasting be your memory, O our sister, who are worthy of blessedness and eternal memory.

Through the prayers of our holy Fathers, Lord, Jesus Christ our God, have mercy and save us. Amen.

Holy God, Holy Mighty, Holy Immortal, have mercy on us.

Then he poured a bottle of red wine over the bones, forming the shape of a cross three times. He continued to recite from the funeral service:

You shall sprinkle me with hyssop and I shall be clean. You shall wash me and I shall be whiter than snow.

The earth is the Lord's, and the fullness thereof; the world, and all that dwell therein. You are dust, and to dust you will return.

While people filed out of the graveyard, the widow who had performed the exhumation placed the box containing Eleni's bones in the ossuary. Her immediate family went directly home. Everyone else gathered in the church courtyard for the distribution of food, which took place in memory of Eleni and in order to ensure the forgiveness of her sins. Distant relatives and friends of the family offered everyone present a small glass of sweet red wine, a handful of *koliva* (boiled wheat mixed with sugar and cinnamon and decorated with nuts and raisins), a slice of bread, a spoonful of honey, and several pastries, sweets, and other candies. Each person who received an offering of food responded with the wish, "May God forgive her" (Plates 22 and 23).

Most of the women then returned to the house of Eleni's parents, where they were offered water, cognac, and candy as they passed through the front door. The guests went upstairs to the formal reception room to greet Eleni's family with the phrase "you have received her well," the same phrase used to greet those who have recently welcomed home relatives returning after a long absence. The house was soon filled with darkly clothed women sitting quietly or talking about the exhumation. After coffee, small biscuits, and pastries were served, the guests again filed past Eleni's family, saying: "You have received her well. Long life to you. Be patient and have courage."

21

As the women walked slowly home through the village streets in groups of two or three, they commented with approval on both the quantity and the quality of food that had been distributed. Such extravagant hospitality was most appropriate for such a tragic death. They were also impressed with the amount of money that had been collected at the exhumation, and they praised Irini's decision to use it to purchase a new metal gate for the graveyard, a gate that would bear Eleni's name and be a monument to her memory.

Many women, however, were surprised and puzzled by the poor condition of Eleni's remains. Why after five years had Eleni's hair and clothes not decomposed? Why were the bones not clean and white? Some women attributed this to natural causes. The grave was very deep. It was in a shaded area near the graveyard wall. The clothes were nylon. Other women disagreed. They believed that a person whose body did not fully decompose and whose bones were black and unclean had committed sins that had not been forgiven. They all knew, though, that Eleni's reputation had been beyond reproach. Her parents were highly respected as well. Someone asked about her grandparents. An older woman nodded knowingly and said that Eleni's grandfather had been a rural policeman and had often been called on to testify in court during disputes over land ownership and property damage. He may have testified falsely on occasion or accepted a bribe. After all, as the proverb says, "The sins of the parents torment their children." The whole discussion was dismissed by one woman with a sweep of her arm and the comment: "We are nothing, nothing at all. May you rest in paradise, Eleni, and may your sins be forgiven."

On the following evening the dark gaping hole in the center of what had once been Eleni's grave was partly filled in. Half-burned candles and withered flowers lay on the mounds of earth that surrounded the grave. The glass case, which had held Eleni's photograph, was broken. Irini arrived at the graveyard carrying a shovel and several candles. After lighting a candle in the ossuary for Eleni, and at the grave of Kostas, she began slowly filling in the grave where she had sat for so long, on so many evenings.

Soon Maria arrived in the graveyard. She sat down on her son's grave and rested her head against the marble headstone. Then she cried out: "Ah! What will happen to me now, Kostas? What can I do? I'm worse off than before. You have died again." She had returned home from the exhumation the day before only to find her grandson gone. Kostas' widow had come to the village by taxi from Elassona and left immediately, taking her son, Kostas' son, away with her on the long trip to Germany.

Irini, shoveling more slowly now, tried to comfort Maria, telling her that although her grandson had gone away, he would someday come back. Then Irini sighed wearily, looked down at the empty grave in front of her, and said: "Eleni, my child, you have gone away too, but you will never come back."

2

THE ANTHROPOLOGY OF DEATH

DEATH-RELATED BELIEFS and practices have long occupied a position of great importance in the anthropological study of religion, for their diversity across cultures stands in sharp contrast to the universality of death itself.[1]

Cultural evolutionists of the late nineteenth and early twentieth centuries, in their attempts to construct grand evolutionary schemes of social development, devoted much attention to mortuary rituals, ancestor worship, and beliefs in an afterlife. Edward Tylor in his *Primitive Culture*, published in 1871, argued that the attempts of primitive peoples to develop a rational response to the threat of

---

[1] In this brief survey of anthropological approaches to the study of death I have drawn on Goody (1962), Huntington and Metcalf (1979), and Fabian (1973).

death, the ultimate limitation on human existence, led to the creation of the concept of the soul and the belief in its continued existence after death. This in turn led to the worship of ancestors and ultimately to "the belief in Spiritual Beings," which for Tylor was the essence of religion itself. According to this view, therefore, the origin of all religious phenomena could be sought in early attempts to cope with death. Sir James Frazer, who shared many of Tylor's theoretical preconceptions, was also interested in the "problem of death" and its importance for understanding the nature of religion. This interest led to the publication between 1913 and 1924 of Frazer's three-volume study, *The Belief in Immortality and the Worship of the Dead*, in which he conducted a worldwide ethnographic survey of the "crude" attempts of "savages" to deal with the threat of death.

The subject of death continued to play an important part in the anthropological study of religion even after the evolutionary approach of Tylor, Frazer, and others had been discredited because of its ethnocentric scheme of universal cultural evolution, its faulty use of the comparative method, and its unsupported speculations concerning the origin of various institutions, beliefs, and practices. In the twentieth century anthropologists interested in the study of religion shifted their attention from its origins and evolution to study instead the basic functions religion serves in human society. The functional approach to religion had its origin in the work of Émile Durkheim, a French sociologist, and was developed further in the work of British social anthropologists. Functionalists, in their attempts to demonstrate how a religious system serves to affirm and preserve the social system by establishing equilibrium and maintaining social solidarity, learned much from the analysis of death-related behavior.

Durkheim, in *The Elementary Forms of the Religious Life*, published in 1912, argued that funeral rites, and other rituals as well, strengthen social ties and reinforce the social structure of a group by calling forth feelings of togetherness and social solidarity. Robert Hertz, a student of Durkheim, whose important essay on death will be discussed in detail in the next chapter, pointed out that the continuity and permanence of a society is threatened by the death of one of its members. At the death of an individual, society, "disturbed by the shock, must gradually regain its balance." It is only through the performance of mortuary rites during the period of mourning following death that society, "its peace recovered, can triumph over death" (Hertz 1960:82, 86).

This functional approach to the study of death-related beliefs and practices also characterized the writings of many British social anthropologists. Radcliffe-Brown, strongly influenced by Durkheim and his school, wrote in his study of the funeral customs of the Andaman Islanders that a person's death "constitutes a partial destruction of the social cohesion, the normal social life is disorganized, the social equilibrium is disturbed. After the death the society has to organize itself anew and reach a new condition of equilibrium" (1933:285). This view, which has been widely accepted by social scientists and has become almost commonplace in popular consciousness, was clearly expressed by another British social anthropologist, Bronislaw Malinowski (1954:53):

> The ceremonial of death which ties the survivors to the body and rivets them to the place of death, the beliefs in the existence of the spirit, in its beneficent influences or malevolent intentions, in the duties of a series of commemorative or sacrificial ceremonies—in all this religion counteracts the centrifugal forces of fear, dismay, demoralization, and provides the most powerful means of reintegration of the group's shaken solidarity and of the re-establishment of its morale.

The functional approach to the study of religion and particularly to the study of death rites has been severely criticized for its inability to deal with social and cultural change. As Clifford Geertz (1973:142–143) and others have convincingly argued, functionalism, with its emphasis on balance, equilibrium, and stability, has failed to explain the dysfunctional aspects of religious behavior and its ability to contribute to the transformation or disintegration of social and cultural systems. What is needed is a more sophisticated approach that makes possible the full appreciation of the role of religion in the creation, development, and communication of systems of meaning. It is only in such a context that the true significance of death-related activities can be understood.

This study of the experience of death in rural Greece is part of a tradition of interpretive anthropology which, following the lead of Clifford Geertz (1973:3–30), adopts a semiotic approach to the study of culture. According to this approach culture is understood to consist of "socially established structures of meaning" embodied in systems of symbols. It is through these structures of meaning, these "webs of significance," that we order our experience and make sense of the world we inhabit. A semiotic conception of culture as patterns or systems of meaning demands that anthropology become an interpretive science whose task is the elucidation of the conceptual world that constitutes one culture (the "other" culture) and its translation into terms comprehensible to a second culture (the anthropologist's culture, "our" culture).[2]

An important principle of such a theory of culture, one whose significance is not always fully appreciated and one which is particularly relevant to the study of death, is that the common-sense reality of everyday life is socially constructed.[3] An individual's culture, the world he inhabits and experiences in a meaningful and ordered manner, is constructed and maintained through a dialectical process in which the individual externalizes his subjective experiences through expression and communication as he interacts with other members of his society. He projects his own meanings into the world around him. Then the products of this process of externalization are objectified and attain a reality, a facticity, that the individual holds to be prior to and independent of his apprehension of them. Finally this reality is reappropriated or internalized. It is transformed once again "from structures of the objective world into structures of the subjective consciousness" (Berger 1969:4).

The reality that every individual constructs must constantly be validated in order for him to continue to inhabit a world that makes sense. The process of world-maintenance, by which an individual's identity and position in society is affirmed, demands regular and continued interaction with other members of society. If a person's relationship with these significant others is interrupted for any length of time, the reality of his world will be threatened and he will be thrown into a state of anomie. Thus a person's sense of identity, his sense of reality, is produced and maintained by an ongoing "conversation" with his significant others. "The plausibility and stability of the world, as socially defined, is dependent upon the strength and continuity of significant relationships in

---

[2] Crick (1976) offers valuable suggestions for the development of a humanistic anthropology whose primary concern is the translation of cultures.

[3] For a full discussion of the notion of the social construction of reality, see Berger and Luckmann (1967), Berger (1969), and Berger and Kellner (1964).

which conversation about this world can be continually carried on" (Berger and Kellner 1964:4).

This conversation takes place in a literal sense when a person talks with significant others. During this conversation each person expresses or externalizes his subjective reality. He objectifies it linguistically by talking about it. It becomes real. However, speech is only one of the many "languages" in which this conversation takes place. All the symbolic systems that constitute a culture, such as myth, ritual, or art, can be seen as languages. In other words, the symbolic systems of a culture communicate; they convey information; they express meaning. The task of the anthropologist is to interpret the meaning of these cultural forms.

Particular attention has been devoted to the study of religious ritual as a symbolic system or language that plays an important role in the construction of any cultural reality and is therefore part of the conversation with significant others discussed above. To quote again from Clifford Geertz (1973:412–453), rituals "talk about" important cultural themes. They are stories people tell themselves about themselves. Using literary analogies rather than conversational ones, Geertz has called ritual performances "metasocial commentaries," "texts within texts" which can be read or interpreted by both the people who perform them and outside observers.[4]

Anthropologists attempting to understand the reality that is constructed and maintained by ritual performances, the telling of myths, and other forms of expressive behavior must somehow interpret the messages that are being communicated by this behavior. The structuralism of Claude Lévi-Strauss has proved to be most useful in learning the language, in breaking the code, in which these messages are sent.[5]

According to Lévi-Strauss, cultural systems are organized into structures so as to constitute codes or languages, just as the sounds and words of a natural spoken language are organized into linguistic structures. The elements that con-

---

[4] On the concept of "textuality" see Eco (1979). For the relevance of this concept to anthropology see Schwimmer (1980).

[5] A good introduction to the work of Claude Lévi-Strauss and to the use of structural analysis in anthropology can be found in Leach (1970 and 1976).

stitute such codes have no meaning as individual units. They acquire meaning only when combined in such a way that they can be discriminated from one another. Meaning depends on contrast, difference, opposition. Two units that contrast with respect to a single dimension or feature form a binary pair. Lévi-Strauss argues that such binary oppositions as nature/culture, male/female, right/left, and life/death constitute the distinctive features of the code through which myths, rituals, and other expressive forms communicate meaning.

In addition, Lévi-Strauss claims that all myths, and by extension all ritual and symbolic systems, involve attempts to resolve the many unwelcome contradictions with which man is confronted. The purpose of myth, in Lévi-Strauss' words, "is to provide a logical model capable of overcoming a contradiction" (1963:229). Since, however, the contradictions dealt with in myth and ritual are real, they cannot actually be overcome. Therefore, mythical thought and ritual performances can only move from the statement of a contradiction or opposition in a strong form to its statement in a weaker or partially mediated form. "Mythical thought always progresses from the awareness of oppositions toward their resolution . . . two opposite terms with no intermediary always tend to be replaced by two equivalent terms which admit of a third one as mediator . . . " (Lévi-Strauss 1963:224).

Since a final resolution of these conflicts can never be achieved, the messages conveyed by symbolic forms must be endlessly repeated, the repetition serving to make apparent the structure of the message. Thus each version of a myth, each episode in a ritual performance, is an attempt to communicate the same message, to resolve the same contradiction. The various versions or the various episodes are to be seen as different transformations of the same underlying logical structure. Ultimately, then, many forms of symbolic expression constitute "speculations," which "in the last analysis do not seek to depict what is real, but to justify the shortcomings of reality, since the extreme positions are only imagined in order to show they are untenable." This constitutes, to paraphrase Lévi-Strauss, an admission that the reality we inhabit is marred by insurmountable contradictions, contradictions that we cannot understand and would prefer to forget (Lévi-Strauss 1967:30).

We are now in a position to examine the significance of death and death-related beliefs and practices. The first point to be considered is the power of death to disrupt the everyday world. As Peter Berger (1969:3–28) has shown, death is an extreme example of a crisis that threatens to bring about the complete collapse of our socially constructed world. Death emphasizes the precarious, unstable quality of our lives. The loss of a significant other threatens the individual with a sense of meaninglessness and disorder because it confronts him with the loss of his sense of reality and identity. One's own death, as well as the death of others, inspires such terror because of its utter and perfect silence.

However, it is clear that in spite of their knowledge of their own mortality the majority of people in all cultures are able to live meaningful lives in socially constructed worlds, which, though at times delicate and fragile, do not collapse. These worlds are maintained in the face of death, suffering, and injustice, which all threaten anomie, by symbolic systems that legitimate, justify, and explain such phenomena. In many societies it is religion that integrates the fact of death into the meaningful order of human existence. It is religion, with its attendant beliefs and practices, which legitimates death and enables the individual "to go on living in society after the death of significant others and to anticipate his own death with, at the very least, terror sufficiently mitigated so as not to paralyze the continued performance of the routines of everyday life" (Berger and Luckmann 1967:101). More specifically, it is the system of death-related practices which overcomes the threat of social paralysis. Death rites are concrete procedures for the maintenance of reality in the face of death. Through the performance of these rituals, those who have confronted death are able to resume their reality-sustaining conversation.

At this point several questions remain. How, in fact, do death rites deal with the threat of death? If they constitute a continuation of this conversation, what is their message—what are they "saying"? And finally, with whom is this conversation conducted?

In cultures throughout the world, the general message encoded in the structure of mortuary rites and communicated during their performance is that death is not the complete and utter annihilation of the individual, that death is not final. These rites tell those who perform them, and other members of society as well, that there is a life after death. There is some aspect of the individual which transcends death and through its immortality allows society's conversation with itself to continue.

31

In the face of death these rites attempt to establish what Geertz (1973:110) has called a religious perspective, in which the ultimate reality of death is denied through reference to a sacred order that transcends everyday experience. But the assertion that death is not final, complete, or all-powerful, which is put forth by the performance of death rites, contrasts sharply with a common-sense perspective in which we accept the world as it appears to us, a world in which the finality of death is all too real. The process of human social life is marked by "a movement back and forth between the religious perspective and the common-sense perspective" (Geertz 1973:119). In so far as the experience of death is concerned, the religious perspective, with its denial of death, is quite painfully contradicted by the common-sense perspective, with its forced acceptance of death. In this case the movement back and forth between these two perspectives is only accomplished with great difficulty.

The religious perspective that is generated by the performance of death rites can be maintained most easily at the level of subjective reality. Subjectively we are able to deny death and maintain the fiction of our own immortality or of the continued existence, in some form, of significant others who have died. However, as this subjective reality is externalized and objectified during the course of social interaction, problems arise; contradictions begin to appear.

An individual who subjectively maintains a religious perspective, in which the death of a particular significant other is denied, is confronted with an objective reality in which the other members of his society, who are still alive and who have not been so powerfully affected by the death, adopt a common-sense perspective toward the death and are able to accept it. The contradiction between the religious perspective and the common-sense perspective, between subjective reality and objective reality, between the denial and the acceptance of death, can never be fully resolved. As far as our experience of death is concerned, the movement between these two perspectives will always be hampered by this contradiction. This results in an ambivalent attitude toward death, one in which we can neither accept nor deny it fully.

THIS STUDY is specifically concerned with the manner in which the death rituals of rural Greece attempt to mediate the opposition between life and death. Three aspects of this mediating process are considered. First, these death rituals are considered as rites of passage. Their structure is examined in order to understand the manner in which they bring about a transition from life to death. The relationships between the three *dramatis personae* who move on their journey through these rites (the corpse, the soul, and the mourners) are also considered. Particular attention is paid to the rite of exhumation, an instance of the rites of secondary treatment of the dead which are found throughout the world. The exhumation can be seen as an attempt to deny death by reversing the process of burial, and thus as an attempted or partial resurrection.

There follows a structural analysis of the rich tradition of Greek funeral laments. The systems of imagery in these laments are examined in order to identify the metaphors used to mediate the opposition between life and death, an opposition that is of central importance in this genre of Greek oral narrative. Marriage and the journey to distant lands are important metaphors for the experience of death, since they involve painful separation. However, they are only partially analogous to death. The separation involved at marriage and at a journey to distant lands, unlike that at death, is not a permanent one. A return is possible; social interaction can be resumed. The analogy between cyclical patterns in the world of nature and the linear progression of human life can be seen as another attempt to mediate the opposition between life and death. Other important systems of imagery involve food, water, and birds, which all have the ability to mediate this opposition by crossing the boundary between the world of the living and the world of the dead.

This study concludes by examining the way in which the performance of death rituals in rural Greece enables the bereaved individual to continue his relationship with the dead. These rites constitute a temporary continuation of the conversation of the bereaved with the deceased, a one-way conversation, perhaps, yet a conversation that is able nevertheless to sustain at least in part the world of the bereaved as it existed prior to the death. During the rites of passage, however, this conversation, which is carried out symbolically in a religious perspective, is gradually brought to an end. A new reality is constructed, one that does not include the deceased, through new conversations with new significant others conducted in the context of a common-sense perspective. In

33

constructing this new reality, these death rituals also shed light on such important themes in rural Greek life as the position of women; patterns of reciprocity, obligation, and inheritance; and the nature of social interaction within the family. Thus the study of death can yield profound insights into the nature of human life itself.

3

DEATH AS PASSAGE

OVER THE COURSE of our lives we move through a fixed system of categories and states: we are born, mature, marry, become parents, grow old, and die. Arnold Van Gennep in *The Rites of Passage* examined the manner in which passage from one state to another is socially marked and celebrated in various cultures throughout the world. Such a passage is not an instantaneous physical event (the moment of birth or the moment of death); it is a gradual social process, which, like a journey from one place to another, often extends over a long period of time.

Van Gennep recognized that all rites of passage, including those marking birth, initiation, marriage, and death, share a common tripartite structure. They are composed of rites of separation, which remove a person from a previously occupied state; rites of transition or liminality; and rites of incorporation, which integrate him into a new state. The structuralist nature of Van Gennep's insights is apparent: the binary opposition between the two social states defined by the rite of passage is mediated by the transitional period. This tripartite structure is illustrated in Figure 1 (after Leach 1976:78).

FIGURE 1

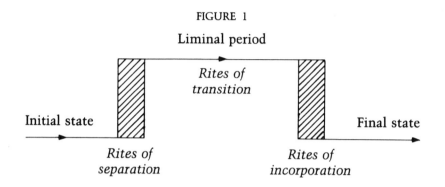

It is important to note that this scheme can often be applied in several different ways to any given sequence of rites marking a passage from one state to another. The first rite of any such sequence can obviously be examined as a rite of separation. However, the same rite may also contain within it features of rites of transition and incorporation, in which case it constitutes a rite of passage in itself and should be analyzed as such. It is not enough simply to apply Van Gennep's scheme to new rituals as one might apply an algebraic formula to new numbers. It is necessary to use Van Gennep's scheme in an original and creative manner in order to achieve new insights into the ethnographic material and in order to understand how the universal structural logic of rites of passage receives expression in the symbolic systems of the particular culture under consideration.

In his discussion of funerals as rites of passage moving people from the world of the living to the world of the dead, Van Gennep points out that although one would expect rites of separation to constitute the most important component of funeral ceremonies, transition rites in fact predominate (1960:146). The period of transition or liminality (from the Latin *limen* meaning "threshold") is the period when the participants in rites of passage are neither in one state nor the other; they are "betwixt and between" (Turner 1967:93–111). They defy classification since they do not fit into any category or position in the social structure.

The liminal period epitomizes that which is ambiguous, paradoxical, and anomalous. As a result, things associated with it are often considered unclean, polluting, and dangerous.

In many societies throughout the world dying is a slow process of transition from one state (life) to another (death). In these societies the burial, which occurs soon after death, is temporary and provisional, and the funeral marks only the beginning of a long and highly elaborated liminal period during which a person is neither fully alive nor fully dead. During this period of transition the corpse decomposes until all the flesh has decayed and only the bones remain. The end of the liminal period is marked by rites of secondary burial or secondary treatment during which the remains of the deceased are recovered, ritually treated, and moved to a new location where they are permanently stored.

The significance of rites of secondary treatment was first noted by Robert Hertz, whose "Contribution to the Study of the Collective Representation of Death" remains one of the most valuable anthropological studies of death. These seemingly bizarre and exotic rites are in fact extremely widespread and can be found in many parts of the world, including North and South America, Africa, Central Asia, Australia, and Indonesia (Hertz 1960:41, Huntington and Metcalf 1979:15).

In his analysis Hertz focuses on three components of the system of beliefs and practices surrounding death, and on the relationships that exist between them. The corpse, the soul, and the mourners are like three actors in a ritual drama, linked symbolically to one another as they move together through the three phases of the rite of passage: separation, transition, and incorporation. The condition of the corpse, which is available for inspection at the rites of secondary treatment, is a model for the condition of the soul. The process of decomposition parallels the journey of the soul to its final destination in the other world. Similarly, the fate of the deceased is paralleled by that of the mourners, who are separated from the rest of society at the moment of death and pass through a liminal period before they are able to re-enter society and resume their normal relationships with others.

The ultimate goal of the rites of passage associated with death is to effect a smooth passage, a successful transition, from one state to another for each of the three actors in this ritual drama. The remains of the dead must be properly disposed of, the soul must arrive at the proper destination, and the mourners must be reincorporated into the flow of everyday social life. Frequently purification is a prerequisite for the accomplishment of these goals. That which is to be transformed from one state to another must first be purified. The corpse must be purified of its decaying flesh, the soul of its sins, and the mourners of their polluting contact with the dead. Separated from the impurities associated with their previous state and with the liminal period, the three actors are incorporated into their new state.

The analysis presented in this chapter draws heavily on Van Gennep's theory of rites of passage and Hertz's study of rites of secondary treatment as well as his insights into the relationships between corpse, soul, and mourners. This analysis is a first step toward understanding the unique manner in which the death rites of rural Greece attempt to mediate the opposition between life and death which confronts us all.[1]

WHEN A GREEK VILLAGER lies at home seriously ill, the Orthodox priest of the village is often invited to the house to perform the sacrament known as the Annointing of the Sick, or Unction. This sacrament contains prayers for the healing of the body and for the purification of the soul through the forgiveness of sins. If death appears imminent, the priest is also asked to offer the sick person communion.

Many people believe that at the moment of death a person's soul (*psihi*), which is described as a breath of air (*mia fisi, enas aeras*) located in the area of the heart, leaves the body through the mouth. Often the moment of death is described in a formalized manner: "He breathed out heavily three times, and his

---

[1] The following account is specifically based on fieldwork conducted in July 1979 in the village of Potamia (a pseudonym, as are the names of all individuals mentioned in this study). In a more general sense this study draws on insights into rural Greek culture gained during fourteen months of fieldwork carried out in Greek Macedonia in 1975–1976 (Danforth 1978). In the transliteration of Greek words and phrases in the text I have been guided by a desire to approximate modern pronunciation. Bibliographical citations, however, are given in more conventional transcription. For other accounts of the manner in which the people of rural Greece deal with death see Alexiou (1974), Megas (1940), and Loukatos (1977:221–225), all of which contain valuable bibliographies.

soul departed." The ease with which the soul is separated from the body is carefully noted. It is highly desirable for the soul to leave the body quickly and painlessly, and a smooth passage is interpreted as a sign that the dying person has led a good life. On the other hand, an agonizingly slow and difficult death is a sign that the departure of the soul is being hindered because the dying person's relationships with the living have been left in an incomplete and unacceptable state. He may have committed a sin against someone which he never confessed, or a person he wronged may not have forgiven him or may have uttered a curse against him. In such cases the dying person is encouraged to confess his sins to a priest, and anyone with whom he has been on bad terms is summoned so that all sins may be forgiven, all curses revoked. Finally, no crying or lamenting is permitted in the presence of the dying person, since that also is believed to hinder the soul's departure from the body. It is significant that the manner in which the soul is separated from the body is closely linked to the manner in which the dying person is separated from the other members of his society. The relationship between the soul and the body is paralleled by the relationship between the dying person and the living.

After death the body is washed and then dressed in new clothes, which many elderly villagers have ready in anticipation of their death. The corpse is laid out on a bed in the formal reception room (saloni) of the house. The feet are tied together, the lower jaw is bound shut, and the eyes are closed. The deceased is then covered up to the waist with a white shroud. After the hands are crossed over the chest and tied together, a large white candle is put between them, and an icon is placed on the legs (Plate 1).

These tasks and the other preparations for the funeral are carried out by women who are either neighbors of the deceased or relatives who are not members of his immediate family. In this way it is possible for the close relatives of the deceased to devote themselves completely to the expression of their grief through crying and singing laments. The female relatives of the deceased put on the black clothes and black kerchief of mourning, changing their own clothes as they changed the clothes of the deceased a short time earlier.

At this point someone is sent to notify the village priest, who arranges for the church bells to be rung slowly in mourning. From the time of death until the funeral, which takes place between twelve and twenty-four hours later, the

39

body is watched over by relatives, neighbors, and fellow villagers in ever increasing numbers. Those who come to pay their respects to the deceased bring candles, which they light and set around his body and in a large tray of flour near the entrance to the room. They place some coins on his chest and kiss both his forehead and the icon on his legs. Finally they shake hands with the close relatives of the deceased and offer them their condolences.

Afterward men usually go out into the hall or the yard, while women are more likely to sit or stand around the corpse and join in the singing of laments (Plate 2). Some people place flowers by the corpse; others leave kerchiefs or towels that will later be distributed to the men who carry the coffin or to those who assist in the funeral in some other way. While relatives from other villages continue to arrive, the grieving reaches new peaks of intensity as people throw themselves over the dead person, hugging him and crying out to him in their pain. In the intervals between the singing of verses of the laments, the close relatives recount the circumstances of the death for each new arrival.

This transitional period between the separation that takes place at death and the funeral itself ends when the village priest arrives. Abruptly the lamenting stops, and all the mourners stand. The priest, holding a lighted candle and a censer, recites the *Trisayio* (Thrice Holy), a portion of the Orthodox funeral service containing prayers for the forgiveness of the sins of the deceased (Plate 3). The body is then taken out of the house into the yard, where it is placed in a simple wooden coffin.

The funeral procession from the home of the deceased to the church is led by two or three women, who carry food and gifts to be distributed after the burial, and several young boys serving as acolytes, who carry a cross and staffs crowned with metal representations of cherubim. They are followed by the priest, the coffin, the immediate family of the deceased, and the other mourners (Plate 5). When the procession arrives at the village church, the coffin is placed in the center of the church with the feet of the deceased toward the altar (Plate 6). The priest then celebrates the Orthodox funeral service, with its poetic yet emphatic call for the quick and successful completion of the passages that constitute death.

The Orthodox funeral service is primarily concerned with the forgiveness of the sins of the deceased, the purification of his soul, and its ultimate incorporation

40

into the appropriate and desired location in the other world. Consider the following prayers from the text of the funeral service:

Give rest to the soul of Your servant, O Savior;
And keep it safe in that life of blessedness
That is lived with You, O Friend of Man. . . .
    Let the Lord God establish his soul where the Just repose. . . .
    O Lord, give rest in a place of light, in a place of green pasture, in a place of refreshment, from where pain and sorrow and mourning have fled away. Every sin by him committed in thought, word, or deed, do You as our Good and Loving God forgive. . . .
    Establish the soul of His servant, departed from us, in the tentings of the Just; give him rest in the bosom of Abraham; and number him among the Just, through His goodness and compassion as our merciful God. . . .
    Give rest, O God, unto Your servant, and appoint for him a place in Paradise; where the choirs of the Saints, O Lord, and the just will shine forth like stars. . . . (Vaporis 1977:99–106)

In addition to these prayers for the incorporation of the soul into paradise, the Orthodox funeral service acknowledges the theme of separation, both as it applies to the departure of the soul from the body and as it applies to the departure of the deceased from his surviving relatives.

    Alas! What an agony the soul endures when from the body it is parting. . . .
    Brethren, come, and let us a farewell kiss give to him whom death has taken, and offer thanks to God. For he has departed from the bosom of his kin. . . . (Vaporis 1977:107, 116)

At this point in the service all those present, led by the priest and the immediate family of the deceased, file past the open coffin, place some coins on the body, and kiss both the icon lying there and the forehead of the deceased (Plate

41

8). This point of separation, like that marked by the departure of the body from the house, is a particularly moving one and evokes the expression of intense grief.

After the funeral service the body is taken to the graveyard, where the hands, feet, and lower jaw of the deceased are untied. Then the open coffin is lowered into the grave (Plates 9–11). The priest pours a bottle of red wine over the body in the form of a cross (Plate 12). He may also do the same with the olive oil and water from the lamp that stood near the body during the vigil in the home of the deceased. At this time he recites the final portion of the funeral service:

> You shall sprinkle me with hyssop and I shall be clean. You shall wash me and I shall be whiter than snow.
> The earth is the Lord's, and the fullness thereof; the world, and all that dwell therein. You are dust, and to dust you will return.
> (Vaporis 1977:118)

Before leaving the grave the priest and all those present toss a handful of earth into the coffin saying, "May God forgive him" (Plate 13). Then the shroud is pulled up over the face of the deceased, the coffin is covered, and the grave is filled (Plates 14–16). The conclusion of the funeral rite is concerned with the incorporation of the corpse into the earth. This is stated clearly in another passage that occurs near the end of the funeral service:

> For consigned to the grave is he; with stone is he to be covered.
> Darkness is his dwelling place; he with the dead is entombed.
> (Vaporis 1977:116)

The immediate family of the deceased return home directly. The others gather in the courtyard of the church outside the graveyard, where *koliva* and bread are distributed. When all have received a handful of *koliva* and a piece of bread and uttered a wish for the forgiveness of the deceased, they return to the house from which the funeral procession set out. Before entering the house, everyone washes his hands and touches a metal tray of smoldering charcoal that lies on the ground in front of the house. None of the food left over from the distribution at the graveyard may be brought back into the house of the deceased.

42

After these rites, which serve to purify the survivors from the pollution associated with death and to mark the separation of the living from the dead, those who have gathered at the house of the deceased are offered water, cigarettes, cognac, and candy. They greet the relatives of the deceased, offer their condolences, and take seats around the tables that now fill most of the rooms of the house.

After coffee and biscuits are served, the priest lights a candle and places it in a tray of *koliva*, beside which are a glass of wine and a slice of bread. The *koliva*, wine, and bread are together known as the *makario* (that which is blessed). After the priest recites a prayer over the *makario*, he distributes it to the close relatives of the deceased to eat. Everyone then repeats the wish that God forgive the deceased. Finally a simple meal is served, usually consisting of rice, potatoes, or beans; olives, cheese, and wine. The next day the female relatives of the deceased wash the house thoroughly. It is also customary at this time to burn or give away the clothes of the deceased. This is done "so that the soul will leave the house."

The funeral rites described here can be seen in an overall perspective as rites of separation which mark the beginning of the long liminal period to follow. This, however, would be an oversimplification. As we have seen, these rites attempt to bring about several types of incorporation as well. In addition to marking the separation of the body from the soul and the dead from the living, these rites express concern for the incorporation of the soul into paradise, the body into the earth, and the close relatives of the deceased back into the world of the living.

The liminal period in these rites lasts from the conclusion of the funeral and burial rites to the rite of exhumation, which in Potamia generally takes place five years later. On the eve of the third day following death, the first in a long series of memorial services, known formally as *mnimosina* (singular *mnimosino*), takes place. Before then no one visits the grave or lights candles there. This three-day period is associated with the three days Christ lay in his tomb prior to his resurrection from the dead. At the memorial service on the third day the female relatives of the deceased gather at the grave for the first time. There, joined by other village women, particularly those in mourning, they cry and sing laments for perhaps an hour (Plates 18 and 19). Then the village priest comes and recites the *Trisayio*. Afterward *koliva* decorated with sugar, raisins, nuts, and spices, as well as bread, pastries, and candy, are distributed in the church courtyard. Finally, at the home of the deceased, guests are served cognac, coffee, biscuits, and candy. In Potamia the same sequence of events is repeated nine days and again six months after the death. Such a rite is commonly referred to simply as a *Trisayio*, or else it is referred to by the date of its occurrence: *stis tris* (at three days), *stis enia* (at nine days), and *sto examino* (at six months).

For forty days following the death, relatives, friends, and neighbors of the deceased visit his immediate family in the evening to bring them a meal and to keep them company. It is said that "they are bringing them comfort" (*tous pi-yenoun parighoria*). During this forty-day period an oil lamp is kept burning twenty-four hours a day in the house of the deceased. On the Saturday evening prior to the fortieth day after death this lamp and a photograph of the deceased are taken from the house and placed on the grave monument, which is always constructed by this time. Then a *Trisayio* is performed at the grave of the deceased (Plates 20 and 21).

The following morning is the occasion for a more elaborate memorial service than those which take place on the third and ninth days. At the completion of the liturgy, performed with bread and wine that have been supplied by the family of the deceased, the priest performs a second *Trisayio* at the grave. Then people return to the church. Here, in the same location where the body of the deceased lay forty days earlier, stands a tray of wheat boiled in milk and sweetened to form a kind of pudding. This pudding, known in Potamia as *panhidha*, is decorated with a cross and the initials of the deceased. Three candles tied together with a black ribbon are lit and placed in the tray. This tray of *panhidha* is referred to as the *makario*, like the plate of *koliva*, bread, and wine at the funeral meal. The mourners stand nearby holding lighted candles as the priest recites the *Trisayio* over the *makario*. Then the *panhidha*, special funeral bread, honey, pastries, candy, and vermouth are distributed outside the church (Plates 22 and 23). Afterward all those present are invited to the house of the deceased, where a meal is served, much like the funeral meal only larger and more elaborate. This meal also includes meat, an indication that the relatives of the deceased, who have not eaten meat since his death, have taken an important step in the process of being reincorporated into normal social life.

This forty-day period, like the three-day period immediately following death,

44

is associated with events in the life of Christ. According to Orthodox tradition, during the forty days after his resurrection Christ appeared to his disciples many times until on the fortieth day he ascended into heaven. This elaborate memorial service held forty days after the death is referred to in Potamia as a *merasma* or *mirasma*, meaning a sharing or a distribution.[2] It is repeated one year after the death. These two rites are also referred to by the date of their occurrence: *stis saranda* (at forty days) and *sto hrono* (at one year).

DURING THE LIMINAL PERIOD following death the surviving relatives are very concerned with the fate of the soul of the deceased. The traditional beliefs held by Greek villagers concerning the soul and the afterlife are an interesting syncretism of Orthodox Christian teachings and various popular beliefs that are remarkably similar to those known to have existed in ancient Greece.[3] When the soul leaves the body at death it is said to have "set out on the road to God" (*kinise ya to dhromo tou theou*). It has been taken away by Haros, a personification of death, who is either identified with the Angel of the Lord (*Angelos Kiriou*), the Archangel Michael, or is believed to be a subordinate of the Archangel and a messenger of God.[4] Some say that the soul remains in the house for three days and wanders on earth until the fortieth day after death. Others say simply that for forty days the soul hovers close to earth visiting the people and places it frequented during life. On the fortieth day the soul is presented by Haros to the Angel of the Lord who takes it to heaven (*stous ouranous*), where it is judged

---

[2] The semantic and etymological associations of the term *mirasma* are revealing. *Mirasma* is derived from *mira*, meaning literally portion or share, and by extension, fate, lot, destiny, even death. *Miroloyi* (plural *miroloyia*), the term for a funeral lament, has been shown to derive from *mira* and *logos* (word, song), and therefore means literally a song to fate (Alexiou 1974:116–118).

[3] For information concerning death-related beliefs and practices in ancient Greece see Kurtz and Boardman (1971) and Vermeule (1979). Early Christian death rituals are discussed in Rush (1941) and Loukatos (1940). On the continuities between ancient and modern Greek death rituals see Alexiou (1974:4–51). A more general treatment of the relationship between the religious beliefs and practices of ancient and modern Greece can be found in Lawson (1910).

[4] On the development of Haros (Charos, or Charon) in Greek tradition see Alexiou (1978).

by God. In other accounts it is the Angel of the Lord or Christ who carries out this judgment.

At the time of judgment the soul is either consigned to paradise (*paradhisos*), a place of light, refreshment, and green pasture (Vaporis 1977:100), or to hell (*kolasi*), a dark, dismal place associated with fire, tar, and torment. Both paradise and hell are vaguely located somewhere in heaven, which is the designation for the other world (*alos kosmos*) that is likely to be used in discussions dealing with the moral condition of the soul and its judgment by God. Another designation for the other world is Hades (*Adhis*), also referred to as the lower world (*kato kosmos*), a gloomy land from which there is no return. Here the souls of the dead lead a pitiful existence with no concern for individual reward or punishment, deprived of food, water, and other necessities and completely dependent upon the living for the fulfillment of all their needs.

The human soul, although deprived at death of its material body, is believed to continue to exist in human form. As the widow who performed Eleni's exhumation put it:

> At death the soul emerges in its entirety, like a man. It has the shape of a man, only it's invisible. It has a mouth and hands and eats real food just like we do. When you see someone in your dreams, it's the soul you see. People in your dreams eat, don't they? The souls of the dead eat too.

She went on to argue that after death a person's soul continues to exhibit the qualities and characteristics that the deceased possessed while alive. She also felt strongly that the souls of the dead are able to see and hear. Therefore they are aware of all the deeds done by the living on their behalf.

This awareness is frequently cited as one of the major reasons for the performance of memorial services during the liminal period after death. These rites are believed to benefit the souls of the dead directly by meeting their needs, needs which they are unable to satisfy themselves in their shadowy existence in the other world. Among the most important of these needs, which the souls of the dead often communicate to the living through dreams, are light, food, water, and clothing. For example, the candles and lamps that are constantly lit in churches

46

and graveyards throughout Greece are believed to help the dead. They are "a prayer for the salvation of the dead." They are lit "so that the souls will have light, so the souls will not remain in the dark." Similarly, the food that is distributed at funerals and memorial services is believed to find its way to the dead. People say: "We distribute food so that the dead will eat, so that the dead will find food in front of them." But the needs of the dead are met not only by the good deeds of the living. They are also met by the good deeds the deceased performed while alive.

In addition to providing for the needs of the souls of the dead, the performance of memorial services is generally believed to assist souls in obtaining forgiveness and in reaching paradise.[5] The importance of obtaining God's blessing and forgiveness is indicated by the two euphemisms most frequently used for the dead person: the forgiven one (o sihoremenos) and the blessed one (o makaritis). Consider the following example of the manner in which the soul of a dead person is believed to be helped by the performance of memorial services and other good deeds:

During the Greek Civil War, which followed World War II, a man murdered a fellow villager. Years later he lay sick and dying, but his soul would not leave his body. He was experiencing a difficult and agonizingly slow death because of the sins he had committed. Finally he died. One of his daughters, Sophia, was very religious. She had many liturgies performed in her father's memory and regularly brought the village priest to her father's grave to perform the Trisayio and to recite prayers for the forgiveness of his sins.

In a dream Sophia once saw the houses in which the dead live in paradise. All the houses were brightly lit, except for one house that was totally dark. It was her father's house. She asked her father why his house was not lit up like the others. He replied: "The time hasn't come yet to put in lights." Sophia understood this to mean that her father's sins had not yet been forgiven. She continued to perform good deeds in

[5] This view is not shared by all Orthodox theologians. There are those who argue that the fate of the soul is sealed at death and that after death there is no possibility of repentance or moral progress. See Ware (1963:259) and Mastrantonis (nd[a]: 8).

order to obtain forgiveness for his sins. The exhumation of his remains was delayed two years for fear that his body had not decomposed fully. However, when his remains were finally exhumed seven years after his death, his bones were found to be clean and white, proof that his sins had been forgiven and that his soul was resting peacefully in paradise. Sophia firmly believes that this improvement in the condition of her father's soul was brought about by her good deeds on his behalf.

The beliefs expressed here, that the living have a responsibility to pray for the souls of the dead and that these prayers are effective in helping them to obtain forgiveness and enter paradise, are expressed in a passage from the Orthodox funeral service in which the deceased addresses the living as follows:

> Therefore I beg you all, and implore you, to offer prayer unceasingly for me to Christ our God, that I be not assigned for my sins to the place of torment; but that He assign me to the place where there is Light of Life. (Vaporis 1977:117)

We have seen how during the liminal period following death the soul of the deceased is gradually separated from the world of the living and passes over into the world of the dead, where, its sins forgiven, it is incorporated into paradise. Moving now in the direction suggested by Hertz's insights into the parallel that exists between the fate of the soul and that of the corpse, we turn to an examination of the process of transition as it is experienced by the body of the deceased.

From the moment of death, when the soul leaves the body and begins its journey to paradise, the body starts another journey, another passage. It begins to decompose, to return to dust, as the last words of the funeral service suggest. The rites of passage associated with death have as one of their goals the rapid and complete dissolution of the body until all flesh has disappeared, leaving only clean white bones. This decomposition must take place naturally. For these reasons the Orthodox Church does not approve of cremation and discourages the use of airtight, metal, or concrete coffins, which delay decomposition (Mastrantonis nd[b]:10). The goal of physical dissolution and the parallel between this process and the experience of the soul is explicitly expressed in the following prayer from the funeral service:

Let the body indeed be dissolved into the elements [out of which it has been compounded], and let the soul be appointed a place in the Choir of the Just. (Vaporis 1977:113)

When the remains of the deceased are exhumed, the reduction of the body to pure white bones, compact and immutable, offers visible evidence that the soul of the deceased has entered paradise. As a person's flesh (the impure, perishable portion of the body) decomposes, his sins are forgiven. At the end of these parallel processes both the body and the soul exist in pure and permanent form.

This symbolic association between the soul and the bones of the deceased is captured in the wonderful ambiguity that exists in the concluding passage of the funeral service, which is recited at the burial, at memorial services, and at the exhumation. In this passage the deceased addresses the priest, who is pouring wine in the shape of a cross over the corpse, the grave, or the recently exhumed bones: "You shall wash me and I shall be whiter than snow" (Vaporis 1977:118). Whiteness here refers metaphorically to the purity of the soul of the deceased and literally to the whiteness of his bones at exhumation. This illustrates forcefully the manner in which two aspects of rural Greek death rites, that concerned with the body and that concerned with the soul, are integrated into one coherent system of ritual and belief.

The process of decomposition which the body undergoes following burial is a form of destruction. However, as Hertz himself pointed out, this destruction is often conceptualized as a transition. Hertz claimed that it is widely believed that a material object must be destroyed in this world in order for it to be transformed and pass on into the next world, where it is reconstructed in altered form. What Hertz (1960:46) referred to as the "spiritual duplicate" of the body, the body as it exists in a transformed state in the other world, is expressed in the rural Greek conception of the soul with invisible human form.

Ideally, during the liminal period following death, the soul, its sins forgiven, journeys to paradise, while the body in the grave decomposes. However, there are occasions when all does not go well, when the desired passage or transition does not take place. In such cases the body does not decompose completely and at the exhumation bits of flesh, hair, and clothing are found. In less serious cases the bones of the deceased lie black and unclean in the grave.

After an exhumation where any of this occurs, the following comments are

49

often heard: "[The bones] didn't come out well" (*Dhe vyikan kala*). "He didn't have a good soul" (*Dhen ihe kali psihi*). "The earth didn't forgive him" (*I yis dhen ton sihorese*). "His sins came out on the remains" (*I amarties tou vyikan sta lipsana*). In other words, the sins of the deceased were exposed and his bad reputation confirmed by the poor condition of his remains.[6] It is also said that an incompletely decomposed body is "an example from God" (*paradhighma ap' to theo*) and "a sign for the world to see" (*simadhi ya na dhi o kosmos*); proof, in other words, that the sins of the deceased have not been forgiven and that his soul has been condemned to hell.

Partial decomposition, and the unfortunate fate of the soul to which it attests, may be attributed to several factors. These same factors are also held responsible for the slow separation of the soul from the body at death. In both cases the proper transition from life to death has been blocked by a lack of harmony in the social relationships that the deceased enjoyed with other members of his community. The corpse may have failed to decompose fully because the deceased himself or one of his ancestors committed a sin that was not forgiven. It is also said that if proper burial rites were not performed, if the deceased was excommunicated by the Orthodox Church, or if he was cursed by someone, his body will not decompose. Curses such as "May the earth not receive you" (*Na mi se dhehti i yis*) and "May you remain undecomposed" (*Na minis aliotos*) express the wish that the passage from life to death not occur properly. They are the exact antithesis of prayers for forgiveness and for the decomposition of the body that are frequently heard at funeral and burial services.

Some villagers, particularly men and younger people, offer a more naturalistic explanation for the fact that some corpses fail to decompose fully. They argue that the condition of the remains when they are exhumed is influenced by drugs taken prior to death, by the quality of the soil, and by other natural factors such as depth, dampness, and shade. Following an exhumation there are likely to be private discussions among small groups of people in which an explanation is sought for the condition of the remains. The relatives and friends of a person whose body did not fully decompose attribute this to natural causes. Those on bad terms with the deceased or his family are eager to lay the blame on any sins he may have committed.

[6] On "metaphors of exposure" see Herzfeld (1979).

50

During the discussions following a particular exhumation evidence from other exhumations is cited in support of one argument or the other. A person who attributes decomposition to natural causes may mention the case of a wicked man whose bones were found to be white and dry. The person who attributes decomposition to moral factors can counter with the argument that the man's children through their good deeds secured the forgiveness of their father's soul. More examples are cited with inconclusive results, and the discussion continues. What is important is that these discussions provide opportunities for the evaluation of the character and reputation of the deceased. Finally, for those who attribute decomposition to moral factors, the exhumation and subsequent discussion constitute a form of social control, since the condition of the bones provides tangible proof in a public context of the ultimate fate of the soul.

The view that the bodies of certain categories of sinners do not decompose receives expression in the official teachings of the Orthodox Church. The Orthodox funeral service itself contains prayers of absolution explicitly concerned with the possibility that the corpse might not decompose completely. It also lists several reasons why this might occur.

> If this servant has incurred the curse of father or mother, or a ban invoked upon himself; or if he has provoked any priest to bitter severity, and from him has incurred a ban unbreakable (*dhesmon aliton*); or if he has incurred a Bishop's very grievous interdict, but through thoughtlessness and heedlessness has failed to obtain forgiveness; do You forgive him . . . and let his body indeed dissolve (*dhialison*) into its elements, but his soul do You appoint to dwell in the tentings of the Saints.
>
> (Vaporis 1977:113–114)

Further on, the funeral service makes reference to the power granted by God through Christ and his disciples to priests which enables them "both to bind (*dhesmin*) and loose (*liin*) the sins of men" so that whatever they "bind" on earth shall be "bound" in heaven and whatever they "loose" on earth shall be "loosed" in heaven (Vaporis 1977:114 and Matthew 18:18).

The terms *lio* and *dhesmo* are used here meaning, respectively, to forgive and not to forgive a person's sins. In other words, if a person's sins have been forgiven by a priest on earth they will be forgiven by God in heaven, and his soul will enter paradise. On the other hand, if a person's sins have not been forgiven by a priest they will not be forgiven by God, and his soul will be condemned to hell. These two verbs, *dhesmo* (literally meaning to bind or tie) and *lio* (to untie or set free) are closely related etymologically to several other words in both New Testament Greek, known as koine (the language still used in all Greek Orthodox services), and modern spoken Greek, known as demotic. The noun *dhesmos* is the word used in the funeral service to refer to the "bond" that unites the body and soul before death. At death this bond is dissolved or broken (*dhialio*, a compound form of *lio*). It is hoped that the soul, its sins forgiven (*lio*), will enter paradise, and the body dissolve (*dhialio*) or break up (*analio*, another compound form of *lio*) into its component elements. If the sins of the soul are bound (*dhesmo*), if they are not forgiven, the body and the soul will separate with difficulty and the body will not decompose. Similarly, if the deceased has incurred a ban of excommunication (*dhesmos*) which remains unrevoked or undissolved (*alitos*, also from *lio*), his soul will not enter paradise, nor will his body decompose.

The ambiguities inherent in the terms *dhesmo* and *lio* and their cognates provide fertile ground for the full development of the symbolic parallel between the "dissolution" of the body and the "absolution" of the soul. *Lio* and its cognates are associated with free and complete passage from this world to the next, both in the material and the spiritual realms. *Dhesmo* and its cognates, on the other hand, are associated with the prevention of this transition.

The images of binding and loosing, which have been discussed here in the context of the Orthodox funeral service, are also prominent in other aspects of rural Greek rites of passage associated with death that are not part of the official church-sanctioned tradition. Just prior to burial the lower jaw, hands, and feet of the deceased are untied. This practice has been explained as follows: "They *untie* them (hands, feet, and lower jaw) because if the deceased is *tied up*, he will not *decompose*." (*ta* linoun *yati an ine* dhemenos o nekros, dhen bori na liosi) (Synkollitis 1934:401–402). Here the process of decomposition is metaphorically linked to the untying or "loosing" of portions of the body of the deceased.[7]

---

[7] The words *lino* (to untie) and *liono* (to dissolve) are the demotic counterparts of the words *lio* and *dhialio*, which are used in the Orthodox funeral service.

At the present time, in the rare event that upon exhumation a body is found partly decomposed, it is simply reburied and the liminal period extended until the body has decomposed completely. During this time additional services are performed in the hope that the soul of the deceased may be forgiven and come to rest finally and peacefully in paradise. In the past, however, partial decomposition was associated with another form of incomplete or imperfect transition. An undecomposed body was not a sign that the soul of the deceased had been consigned to hell but a sign that the soul had not been separated completely from the body and from the world of the living. This presented the possibility that the body might be reanimated either by the soul or by the devil.

The belief in revenants, which in my experience is dismissed as outmoded superstition by most Greek villagers today, was examined in detail by John C. Lawson in his book *Modern Greek Folklore and Ancient Greek Religion* (1910:361–542), based on fieldwork carried out between 1898 and 1900. The body of a person who had become a revenant (*vrikolakas*), rather than decomposing, was said to swell up like a drum. The reanimated body left the grave at night and caused harm to the living, particularly to the relatives of the revenant. A revenant was said to pollute food, damage property, and injure livestock. The same categories of people whose bodies are presently believed to remain undecomposed were in the past believed to be likely candidates for becoming revenants. This included those who had not received full funeral rites, those who had committed suicide or been murdered, those who had been cursed or excommunicated, and those who had lived particularly wicked and immoral lives (Lawson 1910:375–376). Lawson goes on to report that the bodies of suspected revenants were either hacked to pieces or burned.[8]

The belief in revenants once again illustrates the parallel that is believed to exist between the moral condition of the soul of the deceased and the physical condition of his body. It also illustrates the relationship between the incomplete separation of the soul from the body and the incomplete separation of the dead from the living. Finally it emphasizes the potential danger of all that is associated with liminality and transition.

Having examined the fate of the body and the soul during the liminal period

---

[8] For a collection of narratives dealing with revenants see Blum and Blum (1970:70–76).

after death, we now turn to a consideration of the third component of the ritual drama, the bereaved kin of the deceased. The restrictions imposed on mourners are an expression of the fact that they have been separated from society as a whole because they continue to participate in a relationship with the deceased. During the liminal period of mourning they too live in a marginal state midway between the world of the living and the world of the dead.

The most conspicuous feature of death-related behavior in rural Greece is undoubtedly the dress of women in mourning. Women who "are in mourning" (ehoun penthos) dress completely in black. They also wear a black kerchief that covers their hair, forehead, and neck. The length of time a woman wears black is determined primarily by her relationship to the deceased. A widow should wear black for the rest of her life or until she remarries, something she should not do prior to the exhumation of her husband. The mother of a young child who dies should wear black for five years or longer. At the death of a parent or sibling a woman should wear black for a period of one to five years, at the death of a mother-in-law or father-in-law for one year. A woman whose aunt or uncle has died would be expected to wear black for six months, whereas a forty-day mourning period would suffice at the death of a more distant relative. The mourning period is likely to be longer than usual in the case of someone who dies at a very young age or in a particularly tragic manner.

A close female relative of the deceased is expected to perform the required memorial services and care properly for his grave. In Potamia this involves daily visits to the grave from the time of death until the exhumation five years later. Women in mourning, particularly widows, lead extremely restricted lives. They do not go to the city to shop, nor do they attend social events such as village festivals, weddings, baptisms, or the like. Singing (except the singing of laments) and dancing are also inappropriate. Women in mourning do attend death rituals performed for others, since they provide opportunities for the expression of their grief.

The period of mourning ends gradually, as women exchange black for dark blue and brown clothes before returning to the brighter colors of everyday life. There is a great deal of social pressure that serves to enforce these practices very strictly. A woman who stops mourning too quickly or who fails to live up to the expectations of other women in any aspect of her mourning behavior is certain to be the target of much gossip and ill will.

The restrictions placed on men at the death of a relative are much less severe, of much shorter duration, and much less strictly enforced.[9] A man is expected to wear a black strip of cloth around one arm and to refrain from singing and dancing, although he may attend weddings and other celebrations where singing and dancing take place. Men are not involved in performing memorial services or in caring for graves. In addition, widowers may remarry without criticism much more quickly than widows. In Potamia there are several widowers who remarried a little more than forty days after their wives' deaths.

A house in which a person has died is often marked by strips of black cloth placed diagonally across the door and windows. No singing or dancing is allowed in the house, and traditional holidays, such as Easter and Christmas, are not celebrated.

Those in mourning are separated from the world of the living because of their contact with the world of the dead. Their seclusion is not only an expression of their own liminality, but also a reflection of the isolation of the corpse lying buried in the ground. Similarly, the black mourning dress is clearly linked to the "black earth," which has taken away the deceased and is consuming his body. During this liminal period the mourners are isolated socially from the world of the living while they are linked symbolically to the world of the dead. They themselves are socially dead and remain so until the rite of exhumation, when they rejoin the world of the living.

THE GREEK PRACTICE of exhuming the decomposed remains of the dead is a rite of secondary treatment which marks the end of the liminal period for all three *dramatis personae* of the ritual drama. The exhumation confirms the fact that the body, cleansed of flesh through the process of decomposition, has reached a final state that is both pure and permanent. It also confirms the arrival of the soul in its final resting place, paradise. However, the rite of exhumation is not merely confirmatory, as Huntington and Metcalf claim (1979:80–81). It is also instrumental, since it brings the liminal period to a close by separating the remains of the deceased in a dramatic, even violent manner from their temporary place of confinement and incorporating them into their final and permanent

[9] The reasons for the differences between male and female involvement in death-related activities will be examined in Chapter 5.

resting place, the village ossuary. The deposition of the bones in the village ossuary is an expression of their complete incorporation into the world of the dead, while the ossuary itself is a powerful symbol of the ultimate unity of the village dead.

The rite of exhumation, which was described in detail in Chapter 1, is the last important rite that must be performed individually for a particular dead person by his surviving kin.[10] The relationship between the deceased and his relatives is for the most part ended at the exhumation. After this the obligations of the living to the deceased are carried out collectively on occasions that serve to honor all the dead. The most important of these occasions are known as *Psihosavata* (Soul Saturdays or All Souls' Days, singular *Psihosavato*), which occur five times a year on the following dates: the Saturday before the festival of Saint Dhimitrios (October 26), the last two Saturdays of the Carnival period that precedes Lent, the first Saturday of Lent, and the Saturday before Pentecost.

On these days women in rural Greece exchange plates of food with their neighbors and bring offerings of *koliva*, bread, cheese, olives, and fruit to the village church where they are blessed by the priest, who also commemorates the village dead by reciting their names. Afterward the priest recites the *Trisayio* in the ossuary and at the graves. Finally each woman distributes to others the offerings of food she has brought in honor of her dead relatives. Each *Psihosavato* is a collective memorial service performed for all the dead of the community and is very similar to the memorial services performed individually for a dead person prior to his exhumation.[11]

THE DEATH RITES of the village of Potamia, which have been described in detail here, are quite similar to those performed in other parts of rural Greece, but a certain degree of regional variation does exist. The intensity with which the women of Potamia mourn for their dead and the frequency with which they visit the graveyard appear to be somewhat unusual. Whereas in Potamia a close female relative of the deceased visits the grave daily from the time of death until the

[10] Women occasionally light candles in the ossuary or ask a priest to recite a *Trisayio* in memory of someone whose remains have been exhumed and placed in the ossuary.

[11] For an account of the rituals and beliefs associated with the *Psihosavato* immediately preceding Pentecost see Litsas (1976).

exhumation five years later, the more common pattern in rural Greece is for a close female relative to visit the grave at the most once a week (usually on Saturday evenings), or simply at memorial services and *Psihosavato* observances. Similar variation exists in the richness and strength of the tradition of singing laments for the dead.

There is more significant variation, however, with respect to the rite of exhumation and the ultimate disposal of the remains. The exhumation may be performed three, five, or seven years after death. In Potamia, as in much of rural Greece, the exhumed bones are placed in an ossuary (*kimitiri* or *kimisi*), usually a small building located in a corner of the village graveyard. In some areas of Greece, however, the exhumed remains are taken to the village church where they are kept until the following Sunday, when a memorial service is performed after the liturgy. Then the remains are taken in full procession back to the graveyard, where they are reburied in the same grave. In other words, "They perform a funeral for the bones" (*Ta kamnoun kidhia*, Stamouli-Saranti 1929:144). In still other areas exhumations are not performed within a specific time following death. They may be performed any number of years later, when a close relative of the deceased dies. In such cases the remains of the deceased are exhumed and immediately reburied underneath or at the foot of the coffin of the relative who has just died. In some cases exhumations are not performed at all.

There are also important differences between the death rituals of rural Greece and death rituals as they are performed in cities and large towns. In urban contexts funeral homes (*ghrafia teleton*) assume much of the responsibility for making the necessary arrangements (publicity, large flower-wreaths, transportation by hearse, reception at the graveyard after the funeral). The singing of laments is rare, and the expression of grief is less intense than in rural contexts.

In cities and large towns burial plots are not free, as they are in villages. A family may buy a plot outright and construct a family tomb (*ikoyeniakos tafos*), or it may rent a plot by the year. In the first case exhumations are only performed when room must be made in the tomb for an additional corpse. The exhumed remains are then reburied in the family tomb. In the second case the family of the deceased rents the plot, usually for three years, at which time an exhumation is performed and the remains are placed in an ossuary (referred to in urban contexts by the more formal term *osteofilakio*). Rent must be paid there as well. If

57

a family chooses not to pay for space in the ossuary, the bones are disposed of in a large open pit (*honeftirio*). Finally, in cities exhumations are performed by professional gravediggers (*nekrothaftes*) in a small ceremony attended by only a few of the deceased's closest relatives.[12]

IT IS EVIDENT from the exhumation of Eleni (described in Chapter 1) that the rite of exhumation as it is practiced in Potamia and in many areas of rural Greece is associated with a complex set of ambiguous, often contradictory images. First and foremost, the removal of the bones from the grave is viewed as a departure, the culmination of the separation between the dead and the living which began at the time of death and was expressed so powerfully in the funeral and burial rites. As such, this separation is a sad and painful one. The deceased is leaving the "home" he has inhabited since death.[13] The grave, which is largely dismantled at the exhumation, is the place where the mourners visit the deceased and express their grief throughout the liminal period. This last departure is dreaded, for it removes the deceased further by destroying the site of the family's mourning, the last point of contact with the dead relative. The exhumation is therefore a final and complete separation of the dead from the living.

The theme of separation is poignantly expressed in the following two laments, both of which were sung at the exhumation of Eleni:

3

Σαββάτο βράδυ, τὴν Κυριακὴ ὡς τὸ γιόμα,
ν-ὅλοι μὲ διώχνουν κι ὅλοι μὲ λένε: —Φεύγα.
Ν-ὡς κι ἡ μάνα μου, κι αὐτὴ μοῦ λέει: —Φεύγα.
Φεύγω κλαίγοντας καὶ παραπονεμένη.

---

[12] This brief survey is based on personal observation and fieldwork carried out in various cities, towns, and villages throughout Greece, as well as on the following published sources: Farantou (1975), Felouki (1929), Lianidis (1964), Lioudaki (1939), Loli (1974), Megas (1940), Mousaiou-Bouyioukou (1965), Stamouli-Saranti (1929), Synkollitis (1934), and Zafeirakopoulos (1911).

[13] The metaphoric association between the home of the deceased and his grave is indicated by the practice of marking family tombs in urban cemeteries with the word *ikima* (home, house, or dwelling place) followed by the surname of the owners. The association between grave and home is further developed in Chapter 5.

One Saturday evening, one Sunday morning,
everyone is driving me away; everyone is telling me to leave.
Even my mother, even she is telling me to leave.
I am leaving with tears and with a heavy heart.[14]

4

Κίνησαν τὰ καράβια, τὰ Ζαγοριανά.
Κίνησε κι ἡ Ἐλένη μ', πάει στὴν ξενητειά.
Οὐδὲ γράμμα μὲ στέλνει, οὐδὲ ἀντιλογιά.
Μόν' στέλνει ἕνα μαντήλι, μαυρομάντηλο.
—Ἐγώ, μάνα μ', θὰ φύγω, θὰ ξενητευτῶ
πολὺ μακρυὰ στὰ ξένα καὶ δὲν ξαναγυρνῶ.
Τὰ μαῦρα νὰ τὰ φορέσης καὶ τὰ λερὰ βάν'.
Ὄντας κινῶ νὰ ἔρθω, ἀντάρα καὶ βροχές,
κι ὄντας γυρίσω πίσω, ἥλιος καὶ στεριά.

The boats from Zagora have departed.
Eleni has departed also; she has gone to a foreign land.
She sent me no letter; she sent me no reply.
She only sent a kerchief, a black kerchief.
"Mother, I will go away. I will go away to a foreign land,
far away to a distant land, and I will never return.
Put on your black clothes! Put on your dirty clothes!
Whenever I set out for home, I meet rain and mist;
and whenever I turn back to that foreign land, I find sunshine and
   good roads."

Here Eleni, whose remains were being exhumed during the singing of these laments, is described as being driven from her home by her mother and as traveling far away "to a foreign land" from which she will not return.[15] The departure portrayed in these two laments is clearly a sad and extremely undesirable one.

[14] Unless otherwise noted, the laments presented in this study were recorded during fieldwork in Potamia. The translations of these laments and of those from other published sources are my own, unless another translator is cited.

[15] The Greek words that have been translated here as "to a foreign land" are *stin xenitia*

However, the departure that takes place at an exhumation is also portrayed as desirable, as a movement from a negatively valued place to a positively valued one. The remains of the deceased are brought up from the dark, damp earth into the light of day. Consider the following couplet sung as Eleni's skull was being uncovered and removed from the grave:

5

Τώρα κίνησα, τώρα θὰ φύγω
ἀπ' τὴ μαύρη γῆς κι ἀπ' τ' ἀραχνιασμένη.

Now I have set out. Now I am about to depart
from the black and cobwebbed earth.

This upward movement from dark to light is believed to be sought by the dead themselves. Many women report dreams in which a deceased relative appears to them and asks them to perform an exhumation. In one case a man who had died four years earlier appeared repeatedly in his widow's dreams asking, "When will I be set free?" (*Pote tha exeleftherotho?*) This departure from the grave is also desirable because it is said to involve the removal of a great weight from the chest of the deceased.

The exhumation also marks the end of the liminal period of mourning for the close female relatives of the deceased. The passage of the remains from a negative to a positive state is paralleled by the passage of the survivors from a state of mourning to a state in which they are reintegrated into the society of the living. Just as the remains come out to the surface (*vyenoun stin epifania*) at the exhumation, so widows after the exhumation are able to come out into society (*vyenoun exo stin kinonia*).[16] Both the remains of the deceased and women in mourning emerge from a state of confinement and darkness. The deceased leaves behind the black earth, while women in mourning take off their black

---

and *sta xena*. Both terms are derived from the adjective *xenos* (plural *xeni*), denoting something that is foreign, alien, or "other." That which is *xenos* is outside the reference group in question, whether it be a kindred, a village, or a nation.

[16] On the use of the verb *vyeno* see note 6 above.

clothes. Finally the removal of the weight of the earth from the deceased is paralleled by the "lightening" of the "heavy pain" (*varis ponos*) of the mourners.

The use of the term *kimitiri* or *kimisi* to refer to the village ossuary is another indication that the movement of the remains at the rite of exhumation is a desirable and positively valued one. The word *kimitiri* means literally a place for sleeping and is derived from the verb *kimame*, to sleep.[17] What is significant here is that the positive connotation of death as a peaceful sleep is associated with the bones in the ossuary rather than with the undecomposed remains in the grave. The same euphemistic metaphor of death as sleep is found in the funeral service, where "those who have fallen asleep" (*i kekimimeni*) is the usual term for the deceased whose souls have found repose in paradise. Thus while the souls of the deceased "sleep" in paradise, their bones "sleep" in the ossuary. The deceased, then, do not fully sleep until after the exhumation, when they have been completely incorporated into the other world.

As we have seen, the exhumation is associated with images of departure, a departure that is at once both desirable and undesirable. The exhumation marks the complete and final separation of the dead from the living; it brings their relationship to an end. However, in addition to being a separation and a departure, the exhumation is paradoxically an incorporation and a return. The deceased is not only leaving the world of the living, he is coming back to it as well.

It is clear from the manner in which the exhumed bones of the deceased are treated that in some way the deceased is felt to be returning from the underworld to the world he left at burial. The widow who performed the exhumation of Eleni picked up her skull from the earth and greeted it saying, "Welcome, my dear girl" (*Kalos irthes, koritsi mou kalo*). When she handed the skull to Eleni's mother, she said to her, "You have received her well" (*kalos ti dhehtikes*), the phrase addressed to those who have just welcomed relatives returning home from a long trip.

The act of kissing the skull and touching it to one's forehead is also a form of greeting. Traditionally, when a woman, for example, greeted a respected person, such as her father-in-law or a priest, she kissed his hand, touched it to her

---

[17] Note the English word cemetery, which is cognate. The word regularly used in demotic Greek for cemetery or graveyard is *nekrotafio* (from *nekros*, dead, and *tafos*, grave).

forehead, and kissed it again. It is often said that the exhumation provides an opportunity for the living to see the deceased again after a long absence. The exhumation is motivated in part by a desire for the return of the deceased and a resumption of communication with him.

The image of the exhumation as a return of the deceased from the earth and the realm of the dead is expressed most vividly in several laments sung at the exhumation of Eleni. In the following lament Eleni is portrayed as a small bird eagerly greeted by her relatives on her return to the world of the living:

6

Ἕνα πουλάκι διάβαινε ν-ἀπὸ τὸν Κάτω κόσμο.
Τρέχουν μανοῦλες, τὸ ρωτοῦν, 'δερφούλες τὸ 'ξετάζουν:
—Τί χαμπέρια ν-ἤφερες ἀπὸ τὸν Κάτω κόσμο;

A little bird flew out of the underworld.
Mothers run to ask it questions; sisters run to interrogate it:
"What news have you brought us from the underworld?"

In the next lament Eleni is addressed as a partridge, a term of endearment frequently used by her mother throughout her period of mourning. Eleni is questioned by her relatives about her recent experience in the underworld. In her response she expresses her desire to return home to her mother.

7

—Πέρδικα, περδικούλα μου,
μὲ ποιὸν ἐμάλωνες ἐψές;
—Μὲ τὴ μανούλα μάλωνα,
καὶ μὲ τὸ Χάρο δέρνομαν.
Ν' ἄφ'σες με, Χάρε μ', ν' ἄφ'σες με,
νὰ πάω στὴ μανούλα μου,
νὰ τὴ δῶ.

"My partridge, my little partridge,
with whom were you arguing yesterday?"

"I was arguing with my mother.
I was struggling with Haros.
Let me go, Haros! Let me go!
So that I can go to my mother,
so that I can see her again."

In the following lament, sung while Eleni's brothers were greeting her skull,
Eleni calls out to them to assist her in her struggle with Haros. The dead need
the help of their relatives in order to return to the world of the living.

8

Πέρδικα στέκει καὶ λαλεῖ.
Ἑλένη μ' στέκει καὶ λαλεῖ,
καὶ τ' ἀδερφούλια της φωνάζει:
—Ποῦ 'στε ἀδερφούλια; Λᾶτε 'δῶ.
Ν-ὅλοι τουφέκια ρίξετε.
Ἀπ' τὸ Χάρο νὰ μ' ἁρπάξετε.
—Μὴ φοβᾶσαι, Ἑλένη μου.
Ν-ὅλοι τριγύρω εἴμαστε.
Ν-ὅλοι γιὰ σένα κλαίγομε.

A partridge stands and sings.
Eleni stands and sings.
She cries out to her brothers:
"Where are you, brothers? Come here!
Fire your rifles, all of you!
Rescue me from Haros!"
"Don't be afraid, Eleni!
We are all near you.
We are all weeping for you."[18]

[18] The bond expressed in this lament between the dead woman and her brothers is similar
to the bond expressed in a wedding song between a woman who has left home at marriage
and her brothers (Alexiou 1981:4). This lament, in which a dead woman attempts to return
to the upper world with the help of her living brothers, is an interesting transformation

The final lament to be considered here was sung after Eleni's skull had been removed from the grave. The return of the deceased is expressed clearly and concisely: the passage from the world of the dead to the world of the living is brought into sharp focus by the temporal contrast between the immediate past and the present.

9

—Πέρδικα, περδικούλα μου,
γιὰ ποῦ βραδιάστηκες ἐψές;
—'Εψὲς ἤμαν στὴ μαύρη γῆς.
'Απόψ' ἦρθα στὴ μάνα μου,
ν-ἦρθα καὶ στὸν πατέρα μου,
καὶ στὰ καλὰ 'δερφούλια μου.

"My partridge, my little partridge,
where did you sleep last night?"
"Last night I slept in the black earth,
but tonight I have come to my mother.
I have come to my father
and to my dear brothers and sisters."

If the exhumation is in fact a return, as these laments so strongly suggest, it is a reversal of the process of burial. At the burial the corpse moves from above ground to below ground, from light to dark, from the world of the living to the world of the dead. At the exhumation this movement is exactly reversed.

The terms used by Greek villagers to refer to the process of exhumation support the notion that the exhumation is a negative transformation of the burial. *Xestavrono*, the word most frequently heard in Potamia, means literally to un-cross. It is derived from *xe-* (demotic for *ek-*), a prefix comparable to the English "un-" connoting reversal or negation, plus *stavrono* (to cross), the verb used to

---

of the well-known *Song of the Dead Brother* (Politis 1978:140–142), in which a woman who is alive but has left home at marriage attempts to return home with the help of her dead brother. The analogy between marriage and death suggested here will be explored more fully in the next chapter.

64

refer to the crossing of the hands of the deceased at death. To "uncross," therefore, is to reverse the process of crossing which takes place at death. The word *xehono*, meaning to dig up or exhume, derived from *xe-* plus *hono* (to bury), illustrates this same reversal.[19]

The paradoxical and contradictory images of departure and return, separation and reunion, which are associated with the exhumation are also expressed in the comments of people who have recently participated in these rites. One woman reported that prior to the exhumation of her father (the women of Potamia always refer to the exhumation of a person, never to the exhumation of his remains or bones), she was excited and impatient. She felt a sense of eagerness and anticipation. She thought she would see her father again—alive. She thought she would feel joy, but when she saw only his bones, her hopes were crushed. The joy she had anticipated was transformed into grief and pain.

If the departure that occurs at burial is an occasion for grief, then the return that takes place upon exhumation should be an occasion for joy. But an exhumation is not a joyous return, it is a sad return. Like burial it is a time for tears and laments. An exhumation holds out the hope that the living will welcome back the deceased into the world of the living, but the sight of the decomposed remains destroys this illusion. The emptiness of this hope is conveyed by a comment of Eleni's mother, who, after the exhumation of her daughter, was told, "You have received her well." Eleni's mother replied: "What did I receive? What kind of reception, what kind of welcome was that?"

The implication is clear. The rite of exhumation promises to return that which it cannot. It is "disjunctive," in the sense that it ritually declares passage where in fact there is simply the illusion of passage.[20] The rite of exhumation does not return the dead person to the world of the living; it only returns the decomposed body of what had once been a person. This realization is dramatically expressed in another comment made by Eleni's mother: "Look what I put in and look what I took out! I put in a partridge, and I took out bones." Another woman,

---

[19] The term *xenahono*, often used in Potamia to refer to the process of exhumation, was thought by several villagers to be derived from *xe-* plus *hono*. However, it is more correctly derived from *xena-*, a demotic variant of *xana-* (again, for a second time) plus *hono*, and means literally to rebury.

[20] See Crapanzano (1980).

commenting on the grim facts of exhumation, said: "Nothing comes out, nothing at all. A person goes into the ground and out come bones. The soul is left with God, and the bones are left in the ground." The exhumation is a confrontation with the brutal transformation wrought by death and decomposition. The ambiguity presented by the body of someone who has just died (Is it a person still or not?) is cruelly resolved. Here at last is inescapable proof that the person who was buried five years earlier no longer exists. He has been reduced to bones.

EXHUMATION and burial are two important episodes in the rites of passage associated with death in rural Greece. As such, an important logical relationship exists between them. The exhumation is a negative transformation of the burial, which is itself a negation of life. The exhumation is not, however, a negation of death, because the process of decomposition cannot be reversed. Since it is only the bones of the deceased that are exhumed and not the whole person, the exhumation simply continues the process of separation begun at death.

The exhumation is therefore an attempt to mediate the opposition between life and death, to resolve this universal contradiction by denying the finality of death. As a mediator the exhumation is associated with contradictory, equivocal, and ambiguous imagery. It is both a departure and a return, both a continuation and a reversal of the separation that occurs at death. It brings about a state that partakes of both life and death. The exhumed remains are above ground, no longer separated from the world of the living, yet they are only bones. The deceased is still dead. The mediating position of the exhumed remains is represented in Figure 2.

FIGURE 2

LIFE	EXHUMED REMAINS	DEATH
Alive (+)	Not alive (−)	Not alive (−)
Not separated (+)	Not separated (+)	Separated (−)

The exhumation attempts to mediate the opposition between life and death by replacing it with another, weaker opposition: the opposition between existence in this world, the world above ground, and existence in the underworld. This opposition is weaker in the sense that it can actually be mediated. The remains

66

of the deceased can be moved from one pole of the opposition to the other. The exhumation, involving movement from below ground to above, reverses the process of burial. However, because it involves the decomposed remains of a person rather than the person himself, the exhumation cannot reverse the process of dying. It cannot mediate the stronger opposition between life and death. This process of mediation is illustrated in Figure 3.

FIGURE 3

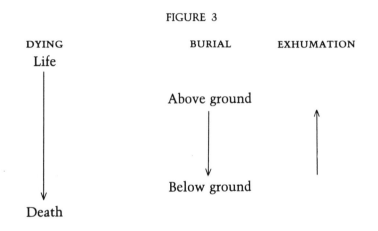

In the last analysis the mediation attempted by the exhumation fails because the contradiction between life and death is real. The exhumation can never bring the dead back to life. Thus the rite of exhumation is finally nothing more than a form of ritual speculation or exploration concerning the possibility of overcoming death.

This is a possibility explicitly held out by the official teachings of the Orthodox Church concerning the bodily resurrection of Christ and the bodily resurrection of all faithful Christians at the Second Coming of Christ. According to Orthodox doctrine, at the Second Coming the souls of the dead will be reunited with their bodies and both the dead and the living will be judged together at the Last Judgment, a collective and final judgment that will reconfirm the individual and partial judgment which takes place after a person's death. The resurrected body, which is to be reunited with the soul, is to be understood not as a material body but as transfigured, spiritual and incorruptible.[21] The resurrected body and the soul will enjoy eternal life in the kingdom of God. However, this mystical belief is rarely mentioned by Greek villagers, and when it is, it is often accompanied by an expression of incredulity and scorn.

The official teachings of the Orthodox Church concerning the resurrection of the dead at the Second Coming actually represent an extrapolation into the realm of mystical belief of the processes of passage, purification, and transformation which have been examined here at the level of popular ritual and belief (see Figure 4). As we have seen, after the separation of the body and soul at death, rural Greek funerary rites attempt to bring about the purification of the soul through the forgiveness of sins as well as the purification of the body through the decomposition of flesh. At the conclusion of the liminal period the rite of exhumation offers proof that the parallel processes of forgiveness and decomposition have been completed, that the spiritual and material components of the person have been purified, and that the cleansed soul and the white bones have achieved a final and permanent state.

Whereas the rite of exhumation reverses the process of burial by removing the material remains of the deceased from the earth, the teachings of the Orthodox Church promise that the body of the deceased will pass completely out of the material world into the spiritual world and be reunited with the soul. In this way the Second Coming will bring to a close the long liminal period during which body and soul have been separated.

The resurrection of the body, however, promises to accomplish something that the rite of exhumation cannot. For even after the exhumation the soul in paradise is still separated from the physical remains of the body on earth. The doctrine of the resurrection promises a complete translation of the body from the material into the spiritual realm and a final reunion with the soul. The dry white bones, the product of decomposition and exhumation, are only an imperfect approximation of the incorruptible spiritual body promised by church teachings.

Thus the doctrines of the resurrection and the Second Coming promise a

[21] This is the official Orthodox version of the "spiritual duplicate" of the body which Hertz (1960:46) claims is brought into existence in the other world when the material body is destroyed. In some respects this conception of the resurrected body corresponds to the popular conception of the soul.

FIGURE 4

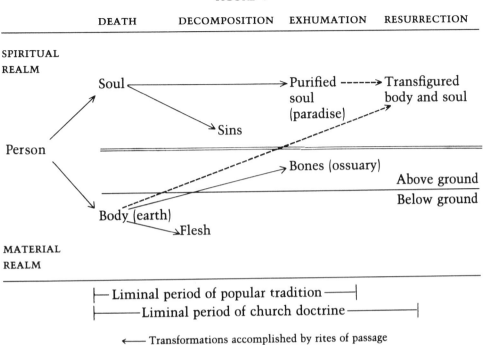

DEATH DECOMPOSITION EXHUMATION RESURRECTION

SPIRITUAL REALM

Soul ⟶ Purified ⤏ Transfigured
soul body and soul
(paradise)

Sins

Person

Bones (ossuary)

Above ground

Below ground

Body (earth)

Flesh

MATERIAL REALM

├─ Liminal period of popular tradition ─┤
├────── Liminal period of church doctrine ──────┤

⟵── Transformations accomplished by rites of passage
⟵ ─ ─ Transformations promised by church doctrine

resolution of the contradiction between life and death. They offer the hope of a successful mediation of the opposition between the material world of the living and the spiritual world of the dead, a true reversal of the process of dying. The resurrection of the dead at the Second Coming constitutes a denial of the ultimate reality and the final power of death. It is a total victory over death.

However, in the world inhabited by Greek villagers, hard white bones are the purest state into which the body can ever actually be transformed. These bones, piled in heaps in ossuaries throughout Greece, testify to the fact that the limits of the material world cannot be transcended. That which has been separated so painfully by death cannot be rejoined. The opposition between life and death inherent in our mortality is real, and the contradiction between our lives and our deaths can never be resolved. What occurs at the rite of exhumation is an imperfect resurrection, at best only a partial victory over death.

4

METAPHORS OF MEDIATION IN GREEK FUNERAL LAMENTS

THE FUNERAL LAMENTS of rural Greece are generally classified as *miroloyia*.[1] In Potamia they are also referred to as *nekratika traghoudhia*, meaning death songs. The most important defining characteristics of these laments are their performance by women at death rituals and their association with the expression of intense grief and sorrow. Greek funeral laments are part of a longstanding oral tradition in which the literary concept of one authentic or correct version of a

[1] The most thorough study of Greek funeral laments is Margaret Alexiou's *The Ritual Lament in Greek Tradition* (1974). See Herzfeld (1981a) for a discussion of the position of *miroloyia* in a taxonomy of rural Greek performative genres.

71

song does not exist. These laments are composed, performed, and transmitted orally. The degree to which each performance is an original creation or composition varies greatly from one region of Greece to another, and, within any region, from one performer to another.[2]

In Potamia, although several women have the ability to compose very original laments, the vast majority of laments sung are well known to most women. In such cases the variation that exists involves the complexity and the degree of elaboration with which traditional themes are presented. In addition, each time a lament is sung, the proper names, kin terms, and descriptive phrases that fit the circumstances of the deceased are inserted in the appropriate places. Thus the formulaic phrase "an old man, a kind father" (*enas yerondas ky enas kalos pateras*) may replace "a youth, a handsome young man" (*enas nioutsikos ky enas kalos levendis*). Similarly, any appropriate proper name or kin term can substitute for "my mother" in the verse "My mother is weeping for me with tears and with pain." Finally, certain laments or themes are only appropriate for certain categories of people. A lament suitable for a young girl who has died would not be sung at the funeral of an elderly widow.

Throughout rural Greece, it is the older women who maintain the tradition of singing laments at funerals, memorial services, and exhumations. Given the rapid rate of urbanization and modernization in Greece, it is not surprising that most younger women do not know laments, do not approve of them, and anticipate that they will not be sung at death rites for which they will be responsible in the future. These young women, who belong to an emerging village middle class with aspirations for a more modern and sophisticated way of life, regard the singing of laments as a source of embarrassment, indicative of rural backwardness and superstition.[3]

Wives, daughters, mothers, and sisters of the deceased, those who are most moved by his death, do not usually lead the singing of laments, because they are too overcome by grief. They spend much of their time crying, sobbing, and calling

[2] On oral composition and transmission generally see Lord (1971). For an application of Lord's ideas to modern Greek folk poetry see Beaton (1980). On authorial originality and creativity see Caraveli-Chaves (1980) and Herzfeld (1981b).

[3] For additional views of the changing social context of Greek funeral laments see Alexiou (1974:50–51) and Caraveli-Chaves (1980:130–131).

72

out to the deceased. The singing is led by women who are less directly touched by the death, more distant relatives of the deceased or women who are not related to him at all. In Potamia these women are not professional mourners in any sense. They are not paid, nor are they even specifically invited to attend a funeral. They are usually women who have become good singers and have learned many laments because they have had much experience with death. Often the women who lead the singing are themselves in mourning and through their singing express their own grief for their own dead.

After the singing of each verse of a lament there is a break during which women whose grief is most intense cry, sob, shout personal messages to the deceased, or talk emotionally about the recent death. When the women who lead the singing begin the next verse they interrupt these cries and shouts. Then those who are most upset pick up the verse and rejoin the singing. In extreme cases, when the close relatives of the deceased continue to cry and shout and do not resume the lament, they may be angrily instructed to do so by other women. For example, at a funeral in Potamia where the widow of the deceased was wildly hugging and kissing her dead husband, her sister, in an attempt to restrain and calm her, spoke to her sharply: "Don't shout like that! Sit down and cry and sing!"

The women of Potamia generally agree that the singing of laments is preferable to wild shouting and wailing as a means of expressing grief at death rituals. Many women believe that such shouting is physically harmful and may cause illness. It is also likely that during this period of uncontrolled shouting the bereaved relative of the deceased may say something inappropriate and embarrassing. She may, for example, reveal information concerning private family matters which would provoke undesirable gossip.[4]

By contrast the singing of laments eliminates the possibility of revealing embarrassing information, since these laments constitute a public language, a cultural code, for the expression of grief. They provide the bereaved with a set of shared symbols, what Lévi-Strauss (1963:199) has called a social myth, which enables them not only to organize their experience of death in a culturally mean-

---

[4] This is an example of the type of exposure involving violation and loss of reputation discussed by Herzfeld (1979:293–294). Compare also the exposure of the sins of the deceased at the exhumation of his undecomposed remains.

ingful way but also to articulate it in a socially approved manner. Women singing laments are communicating in a symbolic language and in the context of a public performance. The goal of a structural analysis of Greek funeral laments is to learn this language in order to understand what is being said about death.

ONE of the most striking features of Greek funeral laments is the close resemblance they bear to the songs that are sung at weddings throughout rural Greece. In Potamia these wedding songs are called *nifika traghoudhia* or *nifiatika traghoudhia*, literally bridal songs. The classification of songs as *miroloyia* or as *nifika traghoudhia* depends on the context in which they are performed. These two categories of songs resemble each other with regard to their musical form, their narrative structure, and their iconography. So close is this resemblance that many songs can be sung at both death rites and weddings. Of such a song it is said: "You can sing it as a funeral lament, and you can also sing it as a wedding song" (*To les miroloyi, to les ke nifiko*). The lyrics and the basic melody of these songs are the same whether they are performed at death rites or at weddings, but the manner in which the melody is sung varies according to the occasion. When these songs are sung at weddings, the style is more forceful, vigorous, and joyful; the melody more elaborate, with trills and light melismatic phrases. At death rites the style is more somber and restrained; the melody flatter and less elaborate.[5]

This relationship between funeral laments and wedding songs is but one aspect of a larger correspondence or analogy between death rites and marriage rites which is to be found in Greek culture. To members of American and Western European cultures the parallel suggested here between marriage and death may at first glance appear startling, since the structural similarities between these rites are largely masked by a cultural emphasis on the differences between them. What two occasions could be more different than the joyful celebration of life that is a wedding and the sad commemoration of death that is a funeral? What could contrast more sharply than the white dress of the bride and the black dress of the widow; the former gaining a husband, the latter losing one? Although it

---

[5] For further discussion of the relationship between *miroloyia* and wedding songs see Alexiou (1974:120–122), Alexiou and Dronke (1971), and Herzfeld (1981a).

is important to bear in mind the logical opposition that exists between these two episodes in the life cycle, it is equally important to understand the no less significant parallels.

Van Gennep (1960:152) and Hertz (1960:81) have both pointed to the similarities that exist between funerals and weddings in cultures throughout the world. Both death and marriage are marked by elaborate rites of passage in which separation is an important theme. The analogy between death and marriage is well developed in ritual and folk song throughout the Balkans (Muşlea 1925) and particularly so in the long tradition of Greek funeral laments (Alexiou 1974, Alexiou and Dronke 1971).

In Potamia, as in most villages of mainland Greece, a bride leaves her home and family of origin at marriage in order to live with her new husband in his father's home. For this reason a woman's wedding, like her funeral, is for her parents and her other close relatives a sad occasion at which her departure evokes the expression of grief.[6] The emotional power of this separation and the psychological distance it introduces between mother and daughter are great, whether the daughter is moving only a few hundred yards away, to the other side of her village, or whether she is leaving her village, and Greece as well, for the United States or Australia. It is therefore not at all surprising that the same songs are sung at both funerals and weddings, that these two rites of passage exhibit many other important similarities, or that the metaphor of death as marriage figures so prominently in Greek folk songs.

The following laments, sung at both funerals and weddings, suggest many of the parallels that exist between these two rites of passage.

10
—Κάτσε, Νίκο μ', ἀκόμ' ἀπόψ',
κι αὔριο πρωὶ νὰ φύγης.
—Τώρα σὲ κάμποσην ὥρα
ὁ χωρισμὸς βαρὺς θὰ γίν'.

---

[6] In discussions of marriage here and elsewhere the perspective of the bride is adopted because it is from this perspective (in a society where residence after marriage is patrilocal) that the analogy between death and marriage is clearest.

Θὰ χωρίσ' ἀπ' τὴν ἀγάπη μ'.
Θὰ χωρίσ' ἀπ' τὸ Δημήτρη μ'.
Θὰ χωρίσ' ἀπ' τὰ ἐγγόνια μ'.

"Stay here, Nikos, just for tonight,
and leave tomorrow morning!"
"In a short time
the painful separation will take place.
I will be separated from my wife.
I will be separated from Dhimitris.
I will be separated from my grandchildren."

In the context of death rites this lament presents Nikos, the deceased, as if he were still alive, anticipating his death and his separation from his wife, his son Dhimitris, and his grandchildren. It is sung at the house of the deceased shortly before the arrival of the village priest just prior to the funeral service. The "painful separation" refers specifically to the imminent removal of Nikos' body from the house. In the context of marriage rites this lament is sung when the groom and his party arrive at the house of the bride to take her to the church for the wedding service. It is at this point that the expression of grief at the departure of the bride is most intense. The name of the bride replaces the name of the deceased in the first line, while "my mother," "my father," and "my brothers and sisters" are inserted in the final lines.

11
Κάτου στὸ Δάφνο ποταμό,
καὶ στὰ δασιὰ τριαντάφυλλα,
ν-ἐκεῖ λαλοῦν τρεῖς πέρδικες.
Καὶ μιὰ πέρδικα δὲ λαλεῖ.
—Γιατί, πέρδικα μ', δὲ λαλεῖς;
—Τί νὰ λαλήσω; Τί νὰ πῶ;
Ν-ἄφησα τὴ μανούλα μου
δίχως καμιὰ παρηγοριά.
Μὴν κλαῖς, μανούλα μου γλυκιά,

καὶ μὴν παραπονιέσαι.
Ἡ τύχη μας τὸ ἔγραψε,
μάνα μ', νὰ χωριστοῦμε.
Σύρι, μάνα μ', στὸ σπίτι μας,
σύρι καὶ στὸ καλό μας.

Down by the river Dhafnos,
by the dense rose bushes,
there three partridges are singing.
But one partridge isn't singing.
"My little partridge, why aren't you singing?"
"Why should I sing? What should I say?
I abandoned my mother
without any solace.
Don't cry, my sweet mother.
Don't have a heavy heart.
Our fate has written
that we must be parted.
Go home, mother.
Farewell!"

This lament, which was sung during the exhumation of Eleni described in Chapter 1, emphasizes the unavoidable nature of the separation that takes place at death. It also suggests the complete break in communication which occurs when the deceased crosses the boundary (suggested perhaps by the river) separating the living from the dead. The deceased is portrayed here as feeling guilty since her death has caused her mother pain. In the context of marriage rites this lament is sung while the bride, the silent partridge, stands, surrounded by her female relatives and friends, awaiting the arrival of the groom to take her away.

12
Ἕνας νέος κι ἕνας καλὸς λεβέντης
μαῦρον τάιζε καὶ μαῦρον μον' ταῖζει
στὰ ψηλὰ βουνά, ψηλὰ στὶς κρύες βρύσες.

—Τρώει ὁ μαῦρος μου τὸ δροσερὸ χορτάρι.
Ἤπιε κρύο νερὸ ἀπὸ τὶς κρύες βρύσες.
Κι αὔριο τὸ πρωί, κι αὔριο τὸ μεσημέρι,
δρόμον ἔχομε κι ἕνα βαρὺ ποτάμι.
Πῶς νὰ διάβομε πέρ' ἀπὸ τὸ ποτάμι;
Ν-ὅλοι πέρασαν πέρ' ἀπὸ τὸ ποτάμι.
Μόν' ὁ νιούτσικος δὲ μπόρεσε νὰ περάσῃ.
Πίσω γύρισε πολὺ μακριὰ στὰ ξένα.

A brave and handsome young man
was feeding his black horse
high in the mountains at cold springs.
"My horse is eating the cool grass.
He is drinking the cold spring water.
Tomorrow morning, tomorrow at noon,
we have a long journey in front of us, and a wide river to cross.
How will we cross over to the other side of the river?"
Everyone crossed over to the other side of the river.
Only the young man was unable to cross.
He turned back; he returned to that foreign land.

When performed at a funeral this lament employs the images of a long journey
and the crossing of a river to represent death. The presentation is somewhat
unusual in that the journey is not a departure from home, nor is it the deceased
who crosses the river, as one might expect. The journey is a return home, while
the deceased is permanently "on the other side of the river," "in a foreign land"
(sta xena).[7] What is emphasized here is the impossibility of overcoming the
separation introduced by death. The river, which symbolizes this separation, is
literally referred to as "heavy" (vari), as is the separation itself in lament 10, line
4. This suggests the power, the emotional or psychological "weight," which this
irreversible separation connotes. At a wedding this lament is sung as the groom

[7] See Chapter 3, note 15.

and his party make their way from the groom's home to that of the bride. It refers to the separation of the groom from his childhood and his status as a single man.

In addition to the parallels between marriage rites and death rites suggested by the existence of songs that are both funeral laments and wedding songs, there are also a great many similarities between the ritual details of weddings and funerals as they are performed in rural Greece. Both are rites of passage that begin with the formal dressing of the central character in the ritual drama, the deceased in the case of the funeral and the bride in the case of the wedding. The relationship between the clothing associated with funerals and the clothing associated with weddings is indicated by an old woman's joking reference to the clothes she had prepared for her funeral as her "dowry." Both sets of clothing accompany a woman through an important rite of passage.

The departure of the bride from her home after the arrival of the groom is analogous to the departure of the deceased from his home after the arrival of the priest. In both cases the principal character in the ritual drama is escorted by relatives and friends from the home to the church in a procession. Wedding processions in Potamia are led by two young men holding large white candles. They are followed by several people carrying baskets full of small packages of candy to be distributed after the wedding. Then come the bride and groom, and their relatives. This procession corresponds quite closely to the funeral procession, composed as it is of acolytes with their staffs, women carrying baskets of *koliva*, the coffin with the body of the deceased, and the bereaved kin. At the conclusion of the wedding service, which, like the funeral, takes place in the center of the village church, all those present, led by the close relatives of the bride and groom, file by the newly married couple, greet them with a kiss, and present them with a gift of money, much as they do at the conclusion of the funeral service. The procession from the church to the house of the groom and the rites of incorporation which take place there correspond to the procession from the church to the graveyard and the rites of burial.

The analogy between marriage and death is even clearer, and is explicitly articulated, at the funeral of an unmarried person. On such occasions people say, "We celebrate the funeral like a wedding" (*Tin kidhia tin kanoume sa ghamo*). In effect, the funeral of an unmarried person becomes his wedding. On such occasions funeral laments that are also wedding songs are particularly appropriate.

They may even be sung in the musical style characteristic of wedding songs. Women say they sing these songs at the death of an unmarried person because they did not have the opportunity to sing them while he was alive. They wish they could have sung them at his wedding, but they could not. Therefore they sing them the last time they see him. As Lawson (1910:556) puts it, "for those who died unwed, death itself was the first and only marriage which they experienced."

In Potamia and in many other areas of Greece a person who dies unmarried is buried dressed in wedding attire. The deceased also wears a wedding crown (Plates 2 and 4), which in some cases is actually placed on his head by his godparent, just as it is during the Orthodox wedding ceremony (Synkollitis 1934:392). If a young woman dies before she marries, pieces of embroidery from her dowry are placed in her coffin. According to one report (Megas 1940:201), in certain areas of Greece a widow traditionally went to the funeral of her husband dressed as a bride. At the funeral of a single person in Potamia the young men who carry the coffin and perform other jobs are called *bratimia*, the term used for the men of honor who assist in the performance of wedding rites.[8]

The analogy between death rites and marriage rites is elaborately developed in the following funeral lament recorded in Potamia:

13

Ἐσεῖς παιδιά μ' βλαχόϊπουλα, ἐσεῖς παιδιὰ καημένα,
ταχιὰ θὰ πᾶτε στὸ χωριό, στὴν ἔρημη πατρίδα.
Τουφέκια νὰ μὴ ρίξετε, τραγούδια νὰ μὴν πῆτε,
νὰ μὴ σᾶς ἀκούσ' τ' ἀδέρφια μ' κι ἡ δόλια ἡ ἀδερφή μ',
νὰ μὴ σᾶς ἀκούσ' ἡ ἀγάπη μ', τὰ δόλια μου τὰ 'γγόνια.
Μὴν πῆτε πὼς σκοτώθηκα, πὼς εἶμαι σκοτωμένος.
Μόν' πῆτε πὼς παντρεύτηκα καὶ πῆρα καλὴ γυναίκα.
Πῆρα τὴν πλάκα πεθερά, τὴ μαύρη γῆς γυναίκα,
κι αὐτὰ τὰ λιανοπέτραδα τά 'χω γυναικαδέρφια.

[8] Muşlea (1925) reports many similar parallels between weddings and funerals in other cultures of the Balkans.

You young shepherds, you unfortunate young men,
tomorrow you will go back to our village, to our desolate homeland.
Don't fire your rifles. Don't sing any songs.
Don't let my brothers and sisters hear you.
Don't let my wife or my poor grandchildren hear you.
Don't tell them that I have been killed.
    Don't tell them that I am dead.
Just tell them that I have married and taken a good wife.
I have taken the tombstone as my mother-in-law, the black earth as
    my wife,
and I have the little pebbles as brothers- and sisters-in-law.[9]

Here the dying man tells his companions to announce his marriage rather than his death to his relatives. The metaphor of death as marriage is then filled out in graphic detail. The weight of the tombstone suggests the oppressive nature of one's relationship with one's mother-in-law, who in Greek folk songs is invariably portrayed as a "wicked" relative. The blackness of the earth anticipates the black dress the man's wife will put on as a result of his marriage to the earth. There is an implicit contrast between this black dress and the white dress she would have worn at her marriage. Finally, the pebbles that become the man's brothers-in-law and sisters-in-law are part of the natural world. Thus the passage of the deceased from home and family to the grave, from a social or cultural state to a natural one, is equated with the passage from one's home and family of origin to the home of one's affines.[10] In another version of this song, also recorded in Potamia, the dying man says that the small pebbles will provide him with people to converse with. The obvious impossibility of this conveys paradoxically the utter separation of the deceased from the world of the living as well as the separation of the bride from her home and family of origin at marriage.

[9] For other versions of this well-known lament see Passow (1972), numbers 38, 65, 152, 180, 364, and 374. See also Herzfeld (1981b:129).

[10] The analogy between the tomb and the home of one's affines is stated explicitly in a lament in which a dying woman asks her fiancé to decorate her tomb as he would have decorated their home of marriage (Passow 1972:268).

81

Just as a man at death is said to take "the black earth" as his wife, so a woman at death is said to take Haros (Politis 1978:224), or less frequently Hades (Passow 1972:265), as her husband. More often Hades, rather than being a personification of death, is simply the name for the underworld, where the marriage takes place (Alexiou and Dronke 1971:846). In these laments the husband is portrayed as an unknown and feared stranger who has snatched the young bride away from her home. The image of marrying a personification of death is also found in the Orthodox funeral service, shorn, however, of its associations with classical mythology. God is asked, "Why were we given up to decay? And why *to death united in wedlock?"* (*sinezefhthimen to thanato*). The answer is simply that it is written. It is the will of God (Vaporis 1977:109).[11]

As we have seen, death is in many important respects both like and unlike marriage. This paradoxical relationship of simultaneous opposition and identity, difference and likeness, is the essence of metaphor. To assert through ritual and song that a funeral is a wedding is to establish a metaphoric relationship between the two rites of passage. This association, like all powerful metaphors, involves the "encapsulation of paradox" (Herzfeld 1979:285). It provides a "perspective by incongruity" (Burke 1954:89–96 and 1964:94–99). It is an "appropriately ill-formed utterance" (Basso 1976:116).

By asserting similarity where there exists difference, by demonstrating identity where there exists opposition, metaphors force us to see things in a different light. They establish relationships between things that were thought to be unrelated. The power of metaphors lies in their ability to change the way we view our world. A metaphor makes something that had been vague more concrete, more sharply defined, and it does so in a specific way, for a particular purpose. According to Fernandez (1971:58) the study of metaphor is the study of "the ways

---

[11] In both ancient and modern Greece the field of dream interpretation provides another context in which to explore the relationship between marriage and death. To dream of one is generally believed to foretell the other. See Lawson (1910:553–554) and Alexiou and Dronke (1971:837–838) for evidence concerning ancient Greece, and Pazinis (nd) for information about dream interpretation in modern Greek culture. Note also the dream seen by Eleni's mother just before her daughter's death (Chapter 1).

in which men are aided in conveying inchoate psychological experiences by appealing to a range of more easily observable and concrete events in other domains of their lives."

Death is perhaps the most "inchoate" experience men confront. As such it would seem to be a particularly suitable subject for metaphor. The metaphoric assertion that death is marriage (and its corollaries, that a funeral is a wedding and that the grave is the home of one's affines) is an attempt to make death more familiar. More importantly, however, the metaphor of death as marriage "moves" death closer to life. It makes death a part of life by identifying it with an experience from life. In doing so it denies the finality and the "otherness" of death. It creates the fiction that death is not the end of life, not a total negation of life.

The metaphor of death as marriage is ultimately an attempt to mediate the opposition between life and death. It attempts to do this by establishing marriage as a mediating term and then asserting that death is marriage, that death is not what it really is, a polar term in the opposition between life and death, but that it is the mediating term. The metaphor of death as marriage "moves" death from the opposite of life to the mediator between life and death, from the antithesis of life to a synthesis of life and death.

Marriage is a most appropriate metaphor to mediate the opposition between life and death because of the paradoxical relationship of similarity and difference which it holds with respect to death. Like death marriage involves departure and separation. However, the departure that takes place at marriage is not as extreme as that which occurs at death. At marriage one does not depart from life, from this world. One simply departs from one's home and family of origin. After marriage, as after death, one is apart; but after marriage, as is not the case after death, one is still alive. Marriage therefore is a kind of half death, a partial death.

Figure 5 illustrates the position of marriage as a mediator between life and death.

FIGURE 5

LIFE	MARRIAGE	DEATH
Alive (+)	Alive (+)	Not alive (−)
Not separated (+)	Separated (−)	Separated (−)

The opposition between life and death can never actually be mediated. The mediation of marriage is only metaphoric. However, the metaphor of marriage introduces or generates a new opposition, the opposition between one's home and family of origin, on one hand, and the home of one's affines, on the other. This opposition is weaker than that between life and death because it can actually be mediated. A return from the home of one's affines to one's family of origin is literally possible, even though one cannot return permanently without seriously interrupting the accepted course of one's life cycle.

The process by which an extreme opposition is mediated metaphorically and replaced by a weaker opposition that can actually be mediated is represented in Figure 6.

FIGURE 6

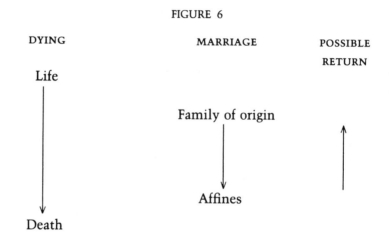

The analysis of the relationship between the funeral and the exhumation presented in Chapter 3 revealed that the return of the deceased from the grave to his home and family, which is ritually attempted at the exhumation, is a negative transformation of his departure from home and family to the grave, which occurs at death. However, this attempt to bring the deceased back to the world of the living is thwarted by the process of decomposition, which transforms a living person into dry bones. The analysis here of the relationship between the

84

funeral and the wedding demonstrates that both rites involve a departure, from home and family to the earth at death, and from home and family of origin to the home of one's affines at marriage. In both cases this movement is portrayed as extremely undesirable, as a movement from good to bad.

Each of the three rites of passage under consideration, the wedding, the funeral, and the exhumation, is an episode in the life cycle of the individual. As such each rite is a "metaphoric transformation" of the other (Leach 1976:25). Having examined two of the three possible relationships between these rites (the relationship between funeral and exhumation and the relationship between funeral and wedding), we now turn to a consideration of the third: the relationship between wedding and exhumation.

AN EXHUMATION is similar to a wedding in several respects. This is particularly true when the person whose remains are exhumed never married. The greeting of the skull at the exhumation by kissing it and placing money on it corresponds remarkably to the greeting the bride and groom receive at the conclusion of the wedding ceremony, when those present greet the newly married couple with a kiss and pin money to their chests. The parallel between exhumation and marriage is also indicated by the wrapping of Eleni's exhumed skull in a kerchief she had embroidered as part of her dowry. Just prior to her exhumation, as people gathered at her house before setting out for the graveyard, several of Eleni's relatives made comments that further emphasized the relationship between her exhumation and her wedding, a wedding that never took place. One of Eleni's sisters said that she planned to place a large sum of money on Eleni's skull (money to be used to build a gate for the graveyard in Eleni's memory) because she would have bought her an expensive gift at her wedding. Eleni's mother complained that more relatives had not come from other villages, adding that if it had been Eleni's wedding more people would certainly have come.

The analogy between exhumation and wedding is also suggested by the fact that the movement in both rites of passage is one of emergence. When the remains of a widow's husband are exhumed, she comes out into society (*vyeni exo stin kinonia*). Similarly, when a woman marries, it is said that she will go out into society (*tha vyi stin kinonia*), or that her husband will take her out into society (*tha tin vgali exo stin kinonia*).[12] Thus just as a woman at marriage emerges into society from the confinement associated with being single, so a widow at the exhumation of her husband's remains re-emerges into society from the confinement of widowhood.

The metaphoric relationship between exhumation and wedding is suggested even more forcefully by the fact that of the sixteen laments sung at Eleni's exhumation, ten were either songs that could be sung at weddings or else versions that had been slightly modified or transformed to render them appropriate for exhumations. Of the seven laments sung at Eleni's exhumation that were presented in Chapter 3, all except one (lament 6) are wedding songs or transformations of them.

In the following discussion of the laments sung at Eleni's exhumation the texts as recorded at the exhumation are presented on the left, while the versions of them that would be sung at a wedding are presented on the right.

<table>
<tr><td>5 (Exhumation)</td><td>5A (Wedding)</td></tr>
<tr><td>Τώρα κίνησα, τώρα θὰ φύγω
ἀπ' τὴ μαύρη γῆς κι ἀπ' τ'
ἀραχνιασμένη.</td><td>Τώρα κίνησα, τώρα θὰ φύγω
ἀπ' τὸ σπίτι μου κι ἀπ' τὰ γλυκά μ' ἀδέρφια.
Ν-ὅλοι μὲ διώχνουν κι ὅλοι μὲ λένε:—Φεύγα.
Ν-ὡς κι ἡ μάνα μου μὲ διώχνει, δὲ μὲ θέλει.
Κι ὁ πατέρας μου, κι αὐτὸς μοῦ λέει:—Φεύγα.
Φεύγω κλαίγοντας καὶ παραπονεμένη.</td></tr>
<tr><td>Now I have set out. Now
   I am about to depart
from the black and cob-
   webbed earth.</td><td>Now I have set out. Now I am
   about to depart
from my home and from my dear
   brothers and sisters.
Everyone is driving me away;
   everyone is telling me to leave.</td></tr>
</table>

[12] The last two examples are from Hirschon (1978:71 and 78). On the emergence of women into public roles associated with the ritual therapy of the Anastenaria see Danforth (1979).

> Even my mother is driving me away.
> She doesn't want me.
> And my father too, even he tells
> me to leave.
> I am leaving with tears and with a
> heavy heart.[13]

Lament 5, sung as Eleni's skull was being uncovered, describes her departure from the earth, a "black," negatively valued place. Lament 5A, which has a melody and a narrative structure very similar to those of lament 5, but which is sung at a wedding rather than at an exhumation, describes the departure of the bride from her home and family of origin. This is obviously a departure from a cherished, positively valued place. Musically and structurally parallel, these songs contrast sharply with respect to content, with respect to the direction of movement. One is a negative transformation of the other.

7 (Exhumation)	7A (Wedding)
—Πέρδικα, περδικούλα μου,	—Πέρδικα, περδικούλα μου,
μὲ ποιὸν ἐμάλωνες ἐψές;	μὲ ποιὸν ἐμάλωνες ἐψές;
—Μὲ τὴ μανούλα μάλωνα,	—Μὲ τὴ μανούλα μάλωνα.
καὶ μὲ τὸ Χάρο δέρνομαν.	Ἰδιώξες με, μάνα μ', 'διώξες με.
Ν' ἄφ'σες με, Χάρε μ', ν' ἄφ'σες με,	Θαρρεῖς θὰ πάνω καὶ θὰ 'ρθῶ,
νὰ πάω στὴ μανούλα μου,	θὰ κάνω χρόνους ἑκατό.
νὰ τὴ δῶ.	Ἐγὼ πίσω δὲν ἔρχομαι.

"My partridge, my little partridge,	"My partridge, my little partridge,
with whom were you arguing yesterday?"	with whom were you arguing yesterday?"

---

[13] Note the similarity between lament 5A and lament 3, which was also sung at Eleni's exhumation.

87

"I was arguing with my
    mother.
I was struggling with
    Haros.
Let me go, Haros! Let
    me go!
So that I can go to my
    mother,
so that I can see her again."

"I was arguing with my
    mother.
You are driving me away, mother.
    You are driving me away.
You think I will go away and come
    back again,
but I will stay away one hundred
    years.
I will never return."

In lament 7 the deceased expresses a desire to escape from the grasp of Haros and to return to her home and her mother. Lament 7A, sung when the groom comes to take the bride to church, portrays an argument between the bride and her mother after which the bride departs, never to return. In lament 7 Haros tries to hold back the person whose remains are being exhumed from the grave, while in lament 7A the bride's mother drives the bride away from her home. The opposition between Haros and the mother, restraint and rejection, grave and home, could not be more vivid.

9 (Exhumation)
—Πέρδικα, περδικούλα μου,
γιὰ ποῦ βραδιάστηκες ἐψές;
—'Εψὲς ἤμαν στὴ μαύρη γῆς.
'Απόψ' ἦρθα στὴ μάνα μου,
ν-ἦρθα καὶ στὸν πατέρα μου,
καὶ στὰ καλὰ 'δερφούλια μου.

"My partridge, my little
    partridge,
where did you sleep last
    night?"
"Last night I slept in the
    black earth,
but tonight I have come to
    my mother.

9A (Wedding)
—Πέρδικα, περδικούλα μου,
γιὰ ποῦ βραδιάστηκες ἐψές;
—'Εψὲς ἤμαν στὴ μάνα μου,
προψὲς στὴν ἀδερφή μου.
Κι ἀπόψ' ἦρθα στὴν ἀφεντιά σ',
ν-ἦρθα στ' ἀρχοντικό μας.

"My partridge, my little
    partridge,
where did you sleep last
    night?"
"Last night I was with my
    mother,
the night before last with
    my sister,

| I have come to my
    father
and to my dear brothers
    and sisters." | but tonight I have come to you,
    mother-in-law,
I have come to our fine
    house." |

These two songs again illustrate the parodoxical relationship of similarity and difference, identity and opposition, which is the essence of metaphor and which characterizes the relationship between the wedding and the exhumation. Lament 9A is sung after the wedding at the door of the house of the groom and his parents, as the mother of the groom greets her new daughter-in-law. The bride responds to her mother-in-law's question with politeness and deference (indicated by the euphemistic reference to her fine new home and the form of address employed—*i afendia s'*). The movement described here, from home and family of origin to the home of the groom, is an unhappy, negatively valued departure. Lament 9, musically and structurally parallel, describes a diametrically opposed movement, a desired return from the grave to home and family of origin.

In the context of an exhumation, the marriage metaphor asserts that an exhumation is a wedding, but it establishes several analogies between the two rites which appear particularly incongruous, paradoxical, and ill-formed. Furthermore, they contradict the analogies established by the same metaphor used in the context of funeral rites.

The funeral-as-wedding metaphor establishes an analogy between a departure from the world of the living for the grave, on one hand, and a departure from one's home and family of origin for the home of one's affines, on the other. The world of the living is like one's home and family of origin (both positively valued), and the grave is like the home of one's affines (both negatively valued). The appropriateness of this metaphor seems clear. The exhumation-as-wedding metaphor, however, establishes an analogy between a return from the grave to the world of the living, on one hand, and a departure from one's home and family of origin for the home of one's affines, on the other. This metaphor asserts paradoxically that the grave is like one's home and family of origin, and the world of the living is like the home of one's affines. Thus the exhumation-as-wedding metaphor seems to contradict the funeral-as-wedding metaphor.[14]

[14] This discussion demonstrates, as Herzfeld (1981b:130) points out, that "symbols do not stand for fixed equivalences, but for contextually comprehensible analogies."

This apparent contradiction recalls the relationship of opposition between the exhumation and the funeral discussed in Chapter 3. The exhumation seems to reverse the movement brought about by the funeral. However, this reversal proves to be illusory, since it is only the dry, white bones of the deceased that return from the earth and not the deceased himself. The exhumation in fact continues the departure that was initiated by the funeral; it does not reverse it.

In effect, the laments sung during Eleni's exhumation assert that the exhumation is a return at the same time as they deny it. Although the lyrics of the laments describe a return, both their musical and narrative structure reveal that what is really taking place is a wedding-like departure. The exhumation-as-wedding metaphor transforms a return into a departure. It asserts that the world of the living to which the deceased appears to have returned is really the home of his affines, that is, the underworld or the grave. It also asserts that the mother to whom the deceased appears to have returned is really his mother-in-law, the heavy tombstone. Thus this metaphor captures the paradoxical nature of the exhumation and conveys to those who perform it the message that the exhumation is not a resurrection. It is a confirmation, not a negation, of death.

The relationships between these three rites of passage, as well as the different movements they bring about, are illustrated in Figure 7. This diagram, modeled after Lévi-Strauss' "culinary triangle" (Lévi-Strauss 1966b and Leach 1970:15–33), demonstrates how the relationships between three terms in a semantic field can be expressed as a double opposition. Here the relationships between wedding, funeral, and exhumation are expressed in terms of the opposition between life and death and the opposition between departure and return. The metaphor of marriage, a rite of passage of the living, is applied to two rites of passage of the dead. This is an attempt to render the inchoate experience of death more accessible and to mediate the opposition between life and death by transforming an experience of the dead into an experience of the living.

ANOTHER important image in Greek funeral laments is that of *xenitia*, a term that refers to foreign or distant lands and the loneliness of living a life of exile there. In addition to being a prominent image in laments, *xenitia* is also very much a psychological and social reality in many parts of Greece at the present time. For years Greeks have left their homes to settle abroad in the United States, Canada, Australia, and more recently Germany, in search of a better standard of

FIGURE 7

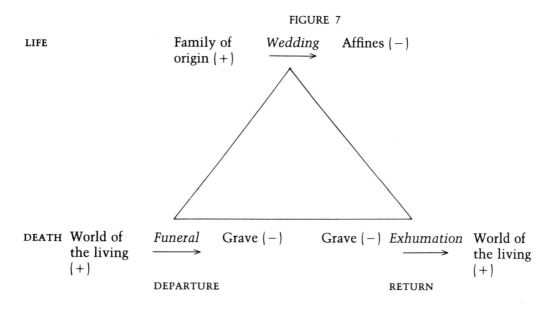

LIFE   Family of   *Wedding*   Affines (−)
        origin (+)   ——————→

DEATH   World of   *Funeral*   Grave (−)   Grave (−)   *Exhumation*   World of
        the living   ——————→   ——————→   the living
        (+)   (+)

        DEPARTURE   RETURN

living for themselves and their families. Virtually everyone in Potamia has a child, sibling, or cousin who is living abroad. *Xenitia* is a recurrent theme in the conversations of the residents of Potamia. Parents discuss the difficulty of not having their children nearby. They often express the fear that one of their children might die in *xenitia*, or that they themselves might die at home alone with all their relatives far away. *Xenitia*, then, like marriage and death, involves a painful departure and a difficult separation from the social network of family, friends, and fellow villagers.

Many songs that can be sung at both weddings and death rituals are songs about *xenitia*. These songs are also sung at family gatherings when close relatives are absent or when someone present is about to depart. Lament 4 is an example of such a song. Here the person living in *xenitia* may represent either the deceased or the bride or groom, depending on the context in which the song is performed. In another version of this song the main character announces that he has married in *xenitia* and will never return home. The departure of a child, particularly a daughter, for *xenitia* at marriage is especially feared.[15]

[15] This theme is celebrated in the *Song of the Dead Brother*. See Chapter 3, note 18.

The following funeral lament is a powerful expression of the metaphor of death as *xenitia*:

14

Βουλιοῦμαι μιά, βουλιοῦμαι δυό, βουλιοῦμαι τρεῖς καὶ πέντε,
βουλιοῦμαι νὰ ξενητευτῶ πολὺ μακριὰ στὰ ξένα.
Ὅσα βουνὰ κι ἂν διαβῶ, ὅλα τὰ παραγγέλνω:
—Βουνὰ νὰ μὴ χιονίσετε, κάμποι μὴν παχνιστῆτε,
ὅσο νὰ πάνω καὶ νὰ 'ρθῶ καὶ πίσω νὰ γυρίσω.
Βρίσκου τὰ χιόνια στὰ βουνά, τοὺς κάμπους παχνιασμένους,
καὶ πάλι πίσω γύρισα στὰ ἔρημα τὰ ξένα.
Γκάμου τοὺς ξένους ἀδελφούς, τὶς ξένες παραμάνες,
γκάμου καὶ μιὰ παραδερφὴ γιὰ νὰ μοῦ πλέν' τὰ ροῦχα.
Τὰ πλένει μιά, τὰ πλένει δυό, τὰ πλένει τρεῖς καὶ πέντε,
κι ἀπὸ τὶς πέντε καὶ μπροστὰ τὰ ρίχνει στὰ σοκάκια.
—Πάρι, ξένη μ', τὰ ροῦχα σου, πάρι καὶ τὰ λερά σου.
Ἐδῶ τοὺς ξένους δὲν τοὺς θέλω, οὐδὲ τοὺς παραχώνω.

Once, twice, three times, five times,
I decided to go far away and live in a foreign land.
I give orders to all the mountains I cross:
"Mountains, don't cover yourselves with snow, plains, don't cover
      yourselves with frost,
until I have gone away and come back home again."
But I find snow on the mountains and frost on the plains,
and I turn back to that desolate foreign land.
I take foreigners as brothers, I take foreigners as foster mothers,
and I take a foreigner as a foster sister to wash my clothes.
She washes them once, twice, three times, five times,
but then she throws them in the streets.
"Foreigner, take your clothes, take your dirty clothes.
I don't want foreigners here, and I don't bury them either."

The desire of the departing person to return home contrasts with the permanence of the separation represented by the barrier of snow and frost (comparable to the barriers of rain and mist in lament 4 and the river in lament 12). In *xenitia* the place of his relatives is taken by *xeni* (foreigners, non-kin).[16] This is the same process that occurs at a woman's marriage, when her affines (who are also referred to as *xeni* in certain contexts) take the place of her family of origin. A metaphoric extension of this process of substituting that which is foreign or "other" for that which is more properly one's own is described in lament 13, where the earth, the tombstone, and small pebbles (inanimate natural objects) take the place of affines (fellow human beings, members of society).

Since he is living in *xenitia*, the central character of lament 14 is deprived of the care and the services his female relatives would provide were he living at home. "Foreign" women are unwilling to fulfill obligations to him that only his family can properly fulfill. It is significant that one of the obligations the foreigners refuse to fulfill is that of providing a proper burial. This emphasizes the desirability of dying at home, where it is certain that one will receive a proper burial at the hands of one's relatives.[17]

The metaphoric relationship between *xenitia* and death involves both similarities and differences. The most obvious of the similarities is that both *xenitia* and death involve departure and separation. This is aptly expressed in a verse from a fifteenth- or sixteenth-century text cited by Politis (1978:195) which states that "*xenitia* and death are considered siblings" (*i xenitia ky o thanatos adhelfia loghounde*). The traditional epithet of *xenitia* is "black," like the black clothes of mourning and the black earth of the grave. One funeral lament states that the person living in *xenitia* should wear black himself (Politis 1978:199). *Xenitia* is also frequently described as "heavy," as are the earth, which weighs down on the chest of the deceased, and the pain that afflicts his relatives.

---

[16] See Chapter 3, note 15.

[17] The type of burial that awaits a person unfortunate enough to die in *xenitia* is described as follows:

> . . . εἴδανε τὰ μάτια μου τοὺς ξένους πῶς τοὺς θάφτουν,
> χωρὶς λιβάνι καὶ κερί, χωρὶς παπᾶ καὶ ψάλτη,
> . . . σὲ χέρισο χωράφι.
> (Passow 1972:271)

My eyes have seen how strangers are buried:
without incense or candles, without a priest or a chanter,
. . . in a fallow field.

Xenitia is often portrayed as "enjoying" the person who lives there, or as "rejoicing" in his presence, in contrast to his relatives at home, who experience anguish and pain (Politis 1978:199).[18] Similarly, the earth is said to "rejoice" in the fact that it consumes those who have died.[19] The analogy between *xenitia* and death is further emphasized in a lament in which a mother of many children states that she does not rejoice, she does not feel joy, because some of her children are in *xenitia* and others have been seized by Haros (Kosmas 1960:369).

The difference between *xenitia* and death is equally apparent, although it is rarely expressed in Greek funeral laments.[20] Death, unlike *xenitia*, involves a permanent separation, from which no return is ever possible. *Xenitia*, however, is often referred to as a living separation (*zondanos horismos*). A person in *xenitia* is still alive, and his relatives may hold out hope for his return.

By virtue of this paradoxical relationship of similarity and difference, *xenitia* is a powerful metaphor for death. This metaphor is a strategic attempt to mediate the opposition between life and death by asserting that death is an experience that partakes of both this world and the other world, thus "moving" death into a mediating position between the two worlds. As *xenitia*, death is not final and can be overcome. It is for this reason that the difference between *xenitia* and death rarely receives expression in Greek funeral laments. The expression of this difference would counteract the movement toward mediation which is such a central feature of the laments.

FIGURE 8

LIFE	XENITIA	DEATH
Alive (+)	Alive (+)	Not alive (−)
Not separated (+)	Separated (−)	Separated (−)

The metaphor of death as *xenitia* also mediates the opposition between life and death by replacing it with the weaker opposition between home and *xenitia*,

---

[18] See also lament 25.　　　　　　　　[19] See lament 18.

[20] The only example of the expression of this difference that I am aware of is contained in a lament in which the deceased tells his children not to make the mistake of thinking that he has only gone to *xenitia*, a destination from which he might return (Kosmas 1960:368).

weaker because a return from *xenitia* is possible whereas a return from death is not. The metaphor of death as *xenitia* is therefore parallel in every respect to the metaphor of death as marriage, as a comparison of Figures 8 and 9 with Figures 5 and 6 indicates.

FIGURE 9

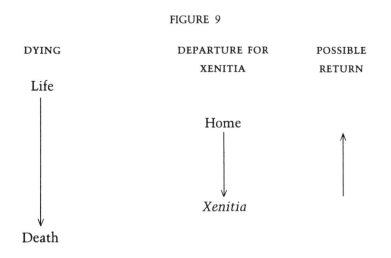

Xenitia and marriage are metaphoric mediators of the opposition between life and death. The rite of exhumation, on the other hand, is an actual or literal attempt to mediate this opposition. The mediation brought about by the rite of exhumation is the inverse of the mediation accomplished by the metaphors of *xenitia* and marriage, since it involves the decomposed remains of people, that is, "people" who are not alive but who are not separated from their home and family. The metaphors of *xenitia* and marriage, when used in this context, evoke people who are alive but who are separated from their home and family of origin. The two forms of mediation, therefore, complement each other. *Xenitia* and marriage preserve life but bring about separation. The exhumation eliminates the separation but harshly demonstrates the loss of life by exposing to public view the decomposed remains of the deceased. These mediations explore all the possibilities of resolving the contradiction between life and death. In the end, however, no complete resolution is possible.

95

GREEK FUNERAL LAMENTS are replete with imagery from the natural world.[21] Through this imagery the human world, the world of culture, on one hand, and the plant world, the world of nature, on the other, are juxtaposed. Most frequently this imagery takes the form of metaphors that equate human beings with plants. Men are identified with tall, strong cypress trees; women with lemon trees and orange trees. People are also equated with apple trees, vines, roses, and other flowers.

The importance of this analogy between culture and nature, human beings and plants, in Greek funeral laments suggests that the opposition between life and death can also be mediated by this metaphor. It is not surprising, then, that death is equated with the uprooting of trees, the burning of gardens, the withering and drying of flowers, and the rotting of fruit. It is often Haros who is responsible for this destruction. Haros burns trees, harvests wheat, picks fruit, and plucks flowers. This imagery is presented concisely in the following couplet:

15
Γιατὶ ὁ κόσμος εἶν' δεντρί, καὶ μεῖς τ' ὀπωρικό του,
κι ὁ Χάρος, ποὺ εἶν' ὁ τρυγητής, μαζώνει τὸν καρπόν του.
(Alexiou 1974:201)

For the world is a tree, and we are its fruit,
and Haros, who is the vintager, gathers its fruit.
(Alexiou)

This metaphor, like the others considered here, is a powerful one because the underlying differences between the two terms, human life and plant life, are only partly masked by the more obvious similarities. As Edmund Leach (1972) has pointed out, human life is a linear process, irreversible and nonrepetitive, moving once and only once from birth to death. Plant life, however, like certain other natural phenomena, involves a process that repeats itself endlessly. In the world of nature life is followed by death, which in turn is followed by rebirth and new life. Plants die only to grow again the following spring. The metaphor of human life as plant life is, therefore, an attempt to deny that human death is final. It is an assertion that human life, like plant life, is repetitive; that there is

[21] See Alexiou (1974:195–201).

life after death. This metaphor seeks to mediate the opposition between human life and death by substituting a weaker opposition, plant life and death. This process is illustrated in Figure 10.

FIGURE 10

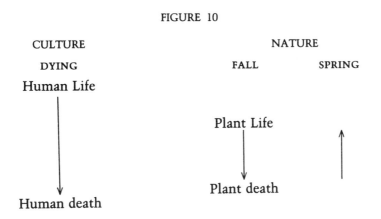

In the plant world death is a prerequisite for the creation of new life. Crops must be harvested and seeds must be planted in order for new crops to grow. This idea is expressed in a biblical passage in which Christ describes human life with imagery from the plant world: "Unless a grain of wheat falls into the earth and dies, it remains alone; but if it dies, it bears much fruit" (John 12:24). This passage is cited by Orthodox priests and scholars in support of the claim that the use of *koliva*, the boiled wheat distributed at death rituals, symbolizes the resurrection of the dead (Mastrantonis nd[b]:10).[22]

Just as reaping and harvesting are common metaphors for death, so planting is a common metaphor for burial. It is this metaphor that organizes both of the following laments:

16
Κυπαρισσάκι μ' ὄμορφο, ποῦ θὲς νὰ σὲ φυτέψω;
Νὰ σὲ φυτέψω στὴν αὐλή; Σκουπίζω, σὲ λερώνω.
Νὰ σὲ φυτέψω στὸ βουνό; Σκιάζομ' ἀπὸ τὸ χιόνι.

[22] George Seferis (1967:359) uses a similar image in his poem *Memory I* when he says, "We are the seed that dies" (*Imaste o sporos pou petheni*).

97

Νὰ σὲ φυτέψω στὸ γιαλό; Σκιάζομ' ἀπὸ τὸ κῦμα.
Νὰ σὲ φυτέψ' σὲ ποταμιά; Γιομίζει καὶ σὲ παίρνει.
Θὲ νὰ σὲ βάλω φύτεμα μέσ' στὸ νεκροταφεῖο,
ν' ἁπλώσῃς κλώνους καὶ κλωνιά, κλώνους καὶ περικλώνια.
Καὶ στὰ περικλωνάρια σου καντήλια θὰ κρεμάσω,
γιὰ νὰ περνᾶνε οἱ φίλοι σου, νὰ τὰ γιομίζουν λάδι,
γιὰ νά 'ρχεται ἡ μανούλα σου, δάκρυα νὰ τὰ γιομίζῃ,
νά 'ρχωνται καὶ τ' ἀδέρφια σου, γιὰ νὰ τ' ἀπογιομίζουν.
(Petropoulos 1959:245)

My beautiful cypress tree, where would you like me to plant you?
Should I plant you in the courtyard? I will sweep there and cover you
    with dust.
Should I plant you on a mountain? I am afraid of the snow.
Should I plant you on the shore? I am afraid of the waves.
Should I plant you in a river bed? Water will rush down and sweep
    you away.
I will plant you in the graveyard,
so that you can spread out your boughs and branches.
On your branches I will hang lamps,
so that your friends can pass by and fill them with oil,
so that your mother can come and fill them with tears,
and so that your brothers and sisters can come and fill them to
    overflowing.

17

Ὁ Χάρος ἐβουλήθηκε νὰ φτιάσῃ περιβόλι.
Τό 'σκαψε, τὸ καλλιέργησε νὰν τὸ δεντροφυτέψῃ.
Φυτεύει νιὲς γιὰ λεμονιές, τοὺς νιοὺς γιὰ κυπαρίσσια,
φύτεψε τὰ μικρὰ παιδιὰ τριαντάφυλλα τρογύρω,
ἔβαλε καὶ τοὺς γέροντες φράχτη στὸ περιβόλι.
(Petropoulos 1959:251)

Haros decided to plant a garden.
He turned over the earth and tilled the soil in order to plant trees.

He planted young women as lemon trees and young men as cypresses.
He planted little children as roses all around,
and he posted old men as a garden fence.

The image of the cypress in lament 16 is a particularly powerful one, since cypress trees have been associated with death and mourning in Greek tradition since antiquity. Cypress trees can now be seen in cemeteries throughout Greece, standing like tall, dark monuments to the dead buried close by.[23] In this lament the planting of a cypress tree is used as a metaphor for burial. The singer is concerned with planting the tree in the appropriate place. When planted in the graveyard the cypress serves as a tombstone, marking the place where the living can come to fulfill their obligations to the deceased.

In lament 17 Haros, who is usually associated with harvesting, an act connoting destruction and death, is represented as planting a garden, an act connoting birth and life. The metaphor of burial as planting suggests that the burial that follows death, like the planting that follows the harvest, will lead to new life. It asserts that burial is a kind of birth.

Plants that are harvested are not all used for replanting. A different fate awaits them, one that also has associations with death. They become food. From destruction and death in the world of nature at harvest comes food, which is consumed by human beings and thus nourishes the human world, the world of culture. Food passes from nature to culture; it mediates the opposition between nature and culture. As Leach (1970:27) has pointed out, "it is . . . a fact that most unprocessed human foodstuffs fall into the category 'domesticated plants and animals,' i.e., they *are* both cultural and natural." When human beings eat products of the earth they are literally establishing an identity between themselves (culture) and their food (nature) (Leach 1970:31). Culture consumes nature. The natural becomes the cultural through the mediation of food.

The relationship between nature and culture, plants and human beings, is developed even further in the symbolic language of Greek funeral laments and death rituals. If plants are food, and if human beings are like plants, then human beings must also, at least in some contexts, be food. It is proof of the internal coherence of the symbolic system under consideration that the metaphor of human beings as food is well developed in the laments.

[23] See Plate 10.

A person's body, which is transformed into a corpse with the departure of his soul at death, becomes food and is consumed by the earth during the rite of burial and the gradual process of decomposition that follows. The image of a human body being eaten by the earth is one of the most graphic and frightening in the entire corpus of Greek funeral laments.

18

Δὲν πρέπει οἱ νιοὶ νὰ χαίρωνται, οὔτε νὰ καμαρώνουν.
Πρέπει ν-ἡ γῆς νὰ χαίρεται κι αὐτὴ νὰ καμαρώνη,
ποὺ τρώει τοὺς νιοὺς καὶ χαίρεται, τὶς νιές καὶ καμαρώνει.
Τρώει ἀγγελικὰ κορμιὰ καὶ πλάτες ἀντρειωμένες,
τρώει μανάδων τὰ παιδιά, τῶν ἀδερφῶν τ' ἀδέρφια,
χωρίζει καὶ τ' ἀντρόγυνα, τὰ πολυαγαπημένα.
(Kosmas 1960:371)

Young men should not rejoice; they should not strut with pride.
Only the earth should rejoice; only the earth should strut with pride,
the earth, which eats young men and rejoices, which eats young
women and is proud.
The earth eats tender bodies and muscular shoulders.
It eats children who have mothers, and brothers who have sisters.
It separates married couples, even those who are very much in love.

This lament emphasizes the pleasure the earth derives from its horrific feast and the pain and suffering it causes the living by eating the dead and depriving the living of their company. The following couplet recorded at a funeral in Potamia focuses on the earth's voracious appetite and the inevitability of being consumed at death.

19

Ἡ γῆς εἶναι ἀχόρταγη. Ποτὲ δὲ θὰ χορτάση.
Γῆς ἀχόρταγη, πόσους ἔφαγες! Κι ἐμένα θὰ μ' ἀφήσης;

The earth is insatiable. It will never be satisfied.
Insatiable earth, how many people you have eaten! You will never let
me go.

Often it is not the earth that eats the corpse but some person or animal closely associated with death and the underworld. In the next two laments it is Haros and a snake who consume the body of the deceased.

20

—Γιὰ πές μου, πές μου, μάτια μου, τὸ πῶς σ' ἐδέχτ' ὁ Χάρος;
—Στὰ γόνατά μου τὸν κρατῶ, στὰ στήθη μ' ἀκουμπάει.
Κι ἂν τὸν πεινάσῃ γιὰ φαγί, τρώγ' ἀπὸ τὸ κορμί μου,
κι ἂν τὸν διψάσῃ γιὰ νερό, πίν' ὀχ τὰ δυό μου μάτια.

(Passow 1972:292)

"Tell me, tell me, my darling: How did Haros receive you?"
"I hold him on my knees. He rests against my chest.
If he is hungry, he eats from my body,
and if he is thirsty, he drinks from my two eyes."

21

—Θέλω κι ἐγώ, παιδάκι μου, κάτι νὰ σὲ ρωτήσω.
Στὸν Κάτω κόσμο πό 'φτασες, πές μου, τ' ηὖρες μπροστά σου;
— Ἐδῶ ποὺ ἦρθα, μάνα μου, ἐδῶ στὸν Κάτω κόσμο,
ηὖρα τὰ φίδια πλεχταριὰ καὶ τὶς ὀχιὲς γαϊτάνι.
Κι ἔνα φιδάκι κολοβό, μικρότερ' ἀπὸ τ' ἄλλα,
φωλίτσα ἦρθε κι ἔφτιασε ἀπάνω στὸ κεφάλι,
καὶ μό 'φαγε τὰ μάτια μου, ποὺ ἤγλεπα τὸν κόσμο.
Μό 'φαγε τὴ γλωσσίτσα μου, τὴν ἀηδονολαλοῦσα,
μό 'φαγε καὶ τὰ χέρια μου, πό 'κανα τὶς δουλειές μου,
μό 'φαγε καὶ τὰ πόδια μου, ποὺ ἐπηγαινορχόμουν.

(Petropoulos 1959:228)

"My little child, I want to ask you something.
Tell me: What did you find waiting for you down in the underworld?"
"Mother, here in the underworld where I have come
I found snakes twisted like braids and vipers curled like ribbons.
One snake, mischievous and smaller than the others,

came and built a nest above my head.
He ate my eyes, with which I saw the world.
He ate my tongue, with which I sang like a nightingale.
He ate my hands, with which I did my chores.
And he ate my feet, with which I used to come and go."

The organs and limbs enumerated in lament 21 are significant in that their destruction highlights the very experiences and activities of life that are taken away at death. Without eyes or tongue, the dead are blind and mute. They are cut off from all forms of communication and social interaction. Without hands, the dead cannot work; without feet, they are rendered immobile. The dead are unable to fulfill their social obligations. In a variant of lament 21 the deceased expresses his fear that he will be eaten by "the worms of Hades," which have gathered around him (Petropoulos 1959:236). In still another variant the deceased implores the tombstone not to eat his red lips or his black eyes (Passow 1972:258). Finally, in a lament in which the deceased dies in *xenitia*, it is "black birds" that eat the corpse (Politis 1978:198).[24]

At death, therefore, the relationship between human beings and the earth, between culture and nature, is reversed. In life people eat the products of the earth. The earth nourishes them. In death, however, their bodies are eaten by the earth. Human beings, transformed into corpses, become food for the earth. While people are alive, then, culture consumes nature, but when they die, nature consumes culture.[25] At death the eater becomes the eaten, and vice versa. This reversal is captured in a phrase uttered, according to Cretan tradition, three times shortly after death: "This very earth which nourished you will eat you as well" (*tout' i yis pou s'ethrepse, touti tha se fai*) (Lioudaki 1939:406).

Whereas food eaten by the living moves from the natural to the cultural, the bodies of the dead, in an inverse transformation, move from the cultural to the natural. This transformation is illustrated by lament 13, in which the deceased

---

[24] Several curses cited by Lawson (1910:388) during a discussion of revenants also involve the metaphor of eating: "May the earth not eat him" (*Na min ton fai to homa*), "May the earth not digest you" (*I yi na mi se honepsi*), and "May the black earth vomit you forth" (*I mavri yi na s'anaxerasi*).

[25] As Lévi-Strauss (1970:219) has said, "death is both *natural* and *anti-cultural*."

marries the earth, takes the tombstone as a mother-in-law, and small pebbles as brothers- and sisters-in-law. Elements of the natural world substitute for those of the social or cultural world. This process of substitution is also illustrated by the following description of a man who died near the ocean far away from his family:

22
Εἶχε τὰ θύκια πάπλωμα καὶ τοὺς ἀφροὺς σεντόνι,
τὰ χοχλιδάκια τοῦ γιαλοῦ εἶχε γιὰ προσκεφάλι.
(Politis 1978:198)

He had seaweed for a blanket and white foam for a sheet,
and a mound of little beach pebbles as a pillow for his head.

Feeding others and exchanging food is an essential feature of social life in rural Greece as it is in cultures throughout the world. Feeding others is central to any offer of hospitality and is the essence of the expression of love and solidarity within the family.[26] As a verse from a lament sung at the death of a woman with children states directly and powerfully, "A mother is sugar, a mother is honey" (*I mana ine zahari, i mana in' to meli*) (Kosmas 1960:368). The contrast between a mother and the earth is expressed in a lament in which the living beg the earth to care for the deceased and to feed him well. The earth replies indignantly that she is not the mother of the deceased but that she is "the black earth" who eats all those who die (Petropoulos 1959:221). A mother feeds the living well. The dead, however, are eaten by the earth.

Just as the metaphor of human life as plant life attempts to mediate the opposition between life and death, so does the metaphor of the human body as food. If the body is eaten by the earth, then it nourishes the earth and gives life to the world of nature. Being eaten, therefore, not only involves destruction and

[26] The importance of food in social relationships in rural Greece is illustrated by the following incident. While trying to persuade her grandson to finish his dinner, a woman said: "When you eat, I'm happy. I love you if you eat, but not if you don't eat." When her grandson refused to eat any more, she asked: "What's the matter? Are you angry with me?"

death; it involves the giving of nourishment and life to that which consumes. If that which dies is really eaten, then from death there emerges life.

The relationships expressed here formally and abstractly in the language of structural analysis are presented more poetically in the following passage from *To chroniko mias politeias* (The Tale of a Town), a novel by Pantelis Prevelakis about the Cretan city of Rethemnos.

> The cemetery of Rethemnos in spring was the most delightful flower garden you will ever see. There were patches of daisies, vines intertwined with honeysuckle, and camomile and mallow spread low along the paths of grass and gravel. Nearby were roses which had flourished boldly over the breasts of the dead, pinks that were redder than blood, begonias, carnations, and rosemary. . . . And you must imagine all this amidst the most sacred silence, with only the buzzing of the bees, those harvesters of the dead who themselves bud and bloom like all things sown.
>
> This sweet metamorphosis, which turns a corpse into honey inside the downy belly of the bee, inspired an enterprising mayor to have a public garden made out of the Turkish cemeteries, after the Turks had left Rethemnos. He knocked over the Turkish tombstones, took away the marble, and plowed up the earth with its dead. The bones came up to the surface, and the rain bleached them white. The gardener went around and plowed the soil again. They sowed it with seed, planted shrubs, laid out flower beds, and dug trenches around the pine trees that had been there during the Turkish period. In short, within one or two years the cemetery had been transformed into a garden. Each root had taken a skull as a breast on which to suck. The trees grew tall, put forth buds and flowers and leaves that rustled in the breeze. The birds heard the noise and hurried to take possession of the garden. They built their nests and burst into song.[27]

Food mediates the opposition between life and death in yet another way. It is believed to cross the boundary between the world of the living and the world

---

[27] In translating this passage I made use of the published translation by Kenneth Johnstone.

of the dead, to pass from this world on over into the other world where the souls of the dead dwell. These souls are thought to have the same needs as living human beings, yet they are unable to satisfy them without help. They are dependent on the living, and on their surviving kin in particular, to provide them with clothes, light, water, and food. In Greek funeral laments the living are often portrayed as sending food to the deceased. In one lament, for example, a dead woman is told to watch for a basket of food which is being sent to her by her living relatives (Kosmas 1960:375).

Women in Potamia hold that the food distributed at memorial services somehow finds its way to the other world, where it is eaten by the dead. They say that the distribution of food takes place "so that the dead may eat" (ya na fan' i pethameni) and that "whatever you give out becomes available for the dead" (afto pou dhinis vriskete ya tous pethamenous). Just as the body of the dead must be destroyed or eaten by the earth in order for it to pass into the other world, so the food distributed at memorial services must be consumed in order for it to reach the dead. Those who eat the food handed out by the relatives of the deceased substitute for the deceased. By consuming this food they enable it to pass into the other world, where it nourishes the dead. A woman whose mother had recently died used to give caramels to people because her mother liked caramels very much. She would tell people, "Here, eat a caramel, so that my mother will eat it."

Everyone who is given food at a memorial service utters a wish that God may forgive the deceased. This practice suggests that food is distributed and eaten not only to feed the dead but also to assure the proper completion of the passage that takes place at death. The soul must be forgiven and enter paradise, while the body must decompose. Thus there is a clear parallel between the consumption of food by the living at the memorial services and the consumption of the body of the deceased by the earth. Both kinds of food, the koliva, panhidha, and bread, on one hand, and the body of the deceased, on the other, must be eaten in order for the soul to enter paradise.

There is additional evidence to support the view that the koliva, panhidha, and bread consumed at death rites are identified symbolically with the body of the deceased. Consider the manner in which the deceased is addressed in the following lament:

105

23

Σταράκι μου καθαριστὸ κι ἀγουροθερισμένο,
ποὺ σ' ἀγουροθερίσανε τοῦ Χάρου οἱ θεριστάδες.

(Alexiou 1974:197)

My little ear of wheat, husked and reaped before your time,
reaped before your time by the reapers of Haros.

Here the deceased is identified with wheat, the primary ingredient in the three most important foods distributed at death rites. *Koliva*, in fact, is often referred to simply as wheat (*sitari*).

There is also a symbolic relationship between the body of the deceased and the *makario*, the tray of *panhidha* distributed at the memorial services forty days and one year after death. In the center of the church the priest blesses the *makario*, which is decorated with a cross, the initials of the deceased, and several candles, just as he performs the funeral service over the body shortly after death. The term *makario* (that which is blessed) is etymologically related to the term *makaritis* (he who is blessed), a common euphemism for the deceased. The *makario* is thus analogous to another symbol that plays a central part in Christian ritual and belief: the bread of communion, a symbol of the body of Christ eaten by Christians everywhere in his memory.

LIKE FOOD, water also mediates the opposition between life and death. It flows from the world of the living to the world of the dead. In the hot, dry climate of Greece water is a powerful symbol of life and all the joys and pleasures associated with it. Cold water flowing from a mountain spring, the epitome of all the good things the dead have left behind, is a common image in Greek funeral laments.[28] In one lament the deceased, as he bids farewell to the world of the living, begs the springs not to run dry, in the hope that one day he might return to drink from them and refresh himself (Kosmas 1960:370). In addition, those who are dying in *xenitia* frequently cry out for water from their homeland.[29]

In contrast to the association between the world of the living and water, the

[28] See lament 12.

world of the dead is associated with thirst, dryness, and heat. As Alexiou points out (1974:203), in Greek funeral laments "the thirsty ones" (*i dhipsasmeni*) is synonymous with "the dead" (*i pethameni*). Hades is a place where those who are thirsty cannot drink (Passow 1972:265). The dead depend on the living to provide them with water as well as food.

Water flows from the world of the living to the world of the dead in many forms. In one lament the deceased prays for rain in order to rot the silk threads that were used to sew his eyes shut. He hopes this will enable him to see the world of the living again (Petropoulos 1959:238). In a lament recorded in Potamia the deceased husband of the singer is described as sleeping. The singer wonders how to wake him and considers offering him a drink of water to bring him back to life.

The pouring of water on the ground or on the grave plays an important part in Greek death rituals. It is reported that in Thrace women traditionally poured water on the ground whenever a funeral procession passed their house. People said that this was done "in order to quench the thirst of the soul of the dead and in order for the dead to drink" (*na dhrosisti i psihi tou nekrou ke na pioun i pethameni*) (Megas 1940:182). Every day the women of Potamia water the flowers on the graves of their dead. The notion that this water somehow reaches the dead is suggested by a good-natured exchange between two widows who were watering the flowers on the graves of their husbands. One widow jokingly accused the other of pouring too much water on the grave. The second widow replied that her husband was buried very deep in the ground and that the water would not reach him. The teasing continued: "Are you trying to drown him? Don't you feel sorry for him?" To which the second widow replied in a more serious tone, "He didn't feel sorry for me when he died."

Death not only imposes a condition of thirst and dryness on the dead. It also places the bereaved in a state associated with heat and lack of water. Death burns. Women in mourning are commonly referred to as burned by death (*harokamenes*). That which is burned turns black, a transformation that is socially marked by the black dress of women in mourning. In a variant of lament 6 the bird that emerges from the underworld has burned wings (Politis 1978:209). Another la-

---

[29] See lament 33.

ment compares both the deceased and a close surviving relative to two trees that have been burned, presumably by Haros (Politis 1978:209). Finally, the emotions aroused by death (grief, pain, and anxiety) are all associated with heat, fire, and flames, and people who experience these emotions are said to be withered or consumed.

Just as death is the absence of life, so dryness and thirst are the absence of water. In a related image, death is associated with poison. In Greek folk songs poison is always a liquid that makes a person thirsty and burns his lips (Ioannou 1970:66). Poison, therefore, is the opposite of water, a negative transformation of water. Water quenches thirst and gives life, but poison burns and causes death. The relationship between death and poison was expressed in one of the most common cries heard at the exhumation of Eleni: "You have poisoned us" (*Mas farmakoses*). The following lament develops even further the notion that the dead have poisoned the living by dying.

24

’Αφήνω γειὰ τὸ σόϊ μου κι ὅλους τοὺς συγγενεῖς μου.
’Αφήνω τὴ μανούλα μου τρία γυαλιὰ φαρμάκι.
Τό ’να νὰ πίνη τὸ πρωί, τ’ ἄλλο τὸ μεσημέρι,
τὸ τρίτο τὸ φαρμακερὸ τὸ βράδυ ποὺ κοιμᾶται.
Μάνα μου, τὰ λουλούδια μου συχνὰ νὰ τὰ ποτίζης,
κάθε πρωὶ μὲ δάκρυα, τὸ βράδυ μὲ τοὺς πόνους.
Κλάψε με, μάνα μ’, κλάψε με.

I bid farewell to my kin, to all my relatives.
I leave my mother three glasses of poison:
the first to drink in the morning, the second to drink at noon,
and the third, the most poisonous, to drink in the evening when she
    lies down to sleep.
Mother, water my flowers often,
every morning with your tears, every evening with your pain.
Weep for me, mother, weep for me.

As the conclusion of this lament suggests, there is yet another liquid that closely attends death: tears, which are both water and poison. Although literally water, tears are described in Greek funeral laments as black, burning, bitter, and poisoned. Their destructive, poisonous quality is conveyed dramatically in the following lament from Potamia:

25

Ξενητεμένο μου πουλὶ καὶ παραπονεμένο,
ἡ ξενητειὰ σὲ χαίρεται κι ἐγὼ πίνω φαρμάκι.
Τί νὰ σοῦ στείλω, Ἑλένη μ'; Τί νὰ σοῦ παραγγείλω;
Νὰ στείλω μῆλο—σέπεται, κυδώνι—μαραγγιάζει.
Νὰ στείλω βασιλικό—δίχως νερὸ στεγνώνει.
Σοῦ στέλνω καὶ τὸ δάκρυ μου σ' ἕνα λινὸ μαντήλι.
Τὸ δάκρυ μ' ἦταν καυτερὸ κι ἔβαψε τὸ μαντήλι.
Σ' ἐννιὰ ποτάμια τό 'πλυνα, δὲ μπόρεσα νὰ τὸ ξεβάψω,
καὶ σ' ἕνα λιανοπόταμο περνῶ καὶ τὸ ξεβάφτω.
Περνάει πέρδικα, πίνει νερό, κι ἔβαψε τὰ φτερά της.

"My little bird, far away in a foreign land, sad and with a heavy heart,
that foreign land rejoices in your presence, and I drink poison.
What should I send you Eleni? What should I order for you?
If I send an apple, it will rot. If I send a quince, it will shrivel up.
If I send basil, without water it will wither.
I will send you a tear in a linen handkerchief."
But my tear was burning hot, and it dyed the handkerchief black.
I washed it in nine rivers, but I could not restore its color.
Then I washed it in a shallow stream, and I did restore its color.
But a partridge flew down to drink from the stream, and its wings
 were dyed black.

This lament expresses the desire on the part of the living to communicate somehow with the deceased, represented here as a little bird in *xenitia*. The singer, Eleni's mother, is poisoned by her daughter's death. She wants to send Eleni food, but she decides against it, because food, like her daughter's body, will decompose. Finally Eleni's mother decides to send a tear, but it is so hot and destructive that it burns the handkerchief and dyes it black. This black stain, like the pain and suffering that accompany death, is difficult to wash away and blackens everything it comes in contact with, even the mottled wings of a beautiful partridge.[30]

Tears, however, are not always poisonous. Like water they can also be life-giving. In lament 24 the deceased gives poison to his living mother and asks for tears in exchange. These tears are the water that nourishes the flowers on his grave. Tears bring comfort to the world of the dead because they represent contact and communication with the world of the living. In a lament from Crete the singer expresses the hope that the tears she sheds will actually resurrect the deceased (Lioudaki 1939:412).

Tears, therefore, are poison in the eyes of the living but water in the world of the dead. Tears are associated with death in this world but with life in the underworld. A transformation from poison to water takes place as tears fall to the ground and sink into the earth. In this way tears mediate both the opposition between life and death and the opposition between water and poison.

26

Γιὰ ἐλᾶτε ξένοι καὶ δικοὶ καὶ ὅλοι οἱ πικραμένοι,
κι ἀπό 'να λόγο πέστε μου κι ἀπό 'να δάκρυ χύστε,
νὰ γένη λίμνη καὶ γιαλός, νὰ γένη κρύα βρύση,
νὰ πάρη τὸν κατήφορο, νὰ πάη στὸν Κάτω κόσμο,
γιὰ νὰ νιφτοῦν οἱ ἄνιφτοι, νὰ πιοῦν οἱ διψασμένοι.
Νὰ πάρ'ν καλὲς νοικοκυρές, νὰ ζυμομαειρέψουν,
τὰ παλληκάρια τὰ καλὰ νὰ φκιάσουν τὸν καρέ τους,
θέλουν νὰ πᾶν περίπατο, νὰ βγοῦνε στὸ σεργιάνι,
καὶ τὰ παιδάκια ἀπ' τὸ σχολειὸ νὰ φκιάσουν τὴ μελάνη.

(Kosmas 1960:374)

Strangers, kinsmen, and all you who grieve, come near.
Say a few words to me and shed a few tears.

---

[30] An interesting transformation of this image can be found in many Greek love songs, where the lips of a lover dye red a kerchief, a river, the ocean, the wings of an eagle, and

So that the tears become a cool spring, a lake, an ocean,
and flood down into the underworld;
so that the unwashed can wash, and the thirsty can drink;
so that good housewives can knead and bake bread;
so that handsome young men can comb and part their hair
when they want to go for a walk, when they want to go out for a
    stroll;
and so that little children in school can make ink to write.

The bitter tears of the living enable the dead to bathe, drink, cook, and make themselves attractive. In other versions of this lament water from the tears of the bereaved is used by the barbers of the underworld as well as by dead women who want to wash their hair and clothes (Petropoulos 1959:217). Tears also provide the dead with ink and thus enable them to communicate with others in writing. In one version of this lament scribes in the underworld, using the tears of the living as ink, write about the pain and the suffering of those who have died (Passow 1972:264).

Occasionally this river of tears is identified with the river that forms the boundary separating the world of the living from the world of the dead.[31] In a lament from Potamia the tears of the living become a flood that uproots trees and threatens to separate violently two brothers who cling to each other as they sit together, like apples, in the branches of an apple tree being swept away by the torrent. In another lament (Passow 1972:264) the river formed by the tears of the living is, like the river Lethe of ancient Greek mythology, a river of forgetfulness, causing those who drink from it to forget their homes and families.

Tears, then, are the ultimate mediator. They both facilitate and block communication. They are both water and poison. Finally, they are able to pass across the boundary between the world of the living and the world of the dead, the very boundary that they may also create. This successive movement from the awareness of strong oppositions toward their resolution by the substitution of weaker oppositions is illustrated in Figure 11.

"half the sun and the entire moon" (Politis 1978:160). Black tears associated with grief are replaced by red lips associated with love, yet the emotion remains equally strong.

  [31] See lament 12.

FIGURE 11

Life

    Wet

        Water

              Tears

       Poison

    Dry

Death

THE OPPOSITION between life and death is mediated in yet another way. Birds, like food and water, are able to cross the boundary between the world of the living and the world of the dead.[32] What is more, as lament 6 indicates, birds are able to cross this boundary in a direction that nothing else can go except revenants: they can return from the world of the dead to the world of the living. They act as messengers who report to the living the condition of the dead in the underworld.

Birds are also able to mediate the opposition between *xenitia* and home, a weakened form of the opposition between the world of the living and the world of the dead. In one lament a young man about to depart for *xenitia* tells his mother that he will depart like the swallows but that unlike the swallows, who will return, he will never come home (Politis 1978:197). The return of such migratory birds as swallows and storks every spring is one of several themes developed in rural Greek rites of passage marking the advent of spring (Herzfeld 1977). As a natural phenomenon that is repeated yearly, this return contrasts sharply with the finality and irreversibility of human death. Because birds are able to return from *xenitia* to their homeland, they are often portrayed as helping people who lie near death in *xenitia* to communicate with their relatives at home. They do this by flying down to the dying man, letting him write a message on their wings, and then taking it to his family (Politis 1978:198).

---

[32] The ability of birds to fly and thus to cross the boundary between this world and the heavens contributes, perhaps, to their appropriateness as mediators of the opposition between this world and the other world.

In addition to mediating the opposition between the world of the living and the world of the dead, birds mediate another opposition that figures prominently in Greek folk songs and in the symbolic systems of cultures throughout the world: the opposition between nature and culture. Birds, as animals, are part of the natural world, yet in Greek folk songs a metaphorical relationship is established between birds and human beings. This relationship involves both differences and similarities. Birds "are feathered, winged, oviparous and they are also physically separated from human society," yet they build homes in which they raise their young, engage in social relationships, and communicate "by acoustic means recalling articulated language" (Lévi-Strauss 1966a:204). Thus the metaphor of human beings as birds mediates the opposition between nature and culture by creating an intermediate category of "natural men" or "cultural animals." It also mediates the opposition between life and death because the assertion that men are birds suggests that men too may come and go, as birds do, between *xenitia* and home, between the world of the living and the world of the dead.

The metaphor of human beings as birds is a common one in Greek funeral laments and Greek folk songs in general. Young women are often referred to in laments as partridges, while young men are represented as eagles (Petropoulos 1959:243). In lament 25 the deceased is portrayed simply as a little bird. Frequently the first appearance in a folk song of a bird who is to play an important role in the narrative is accompanied by the following couplet:

27
Δὲν ἐκελάϊδε σὰν πουλί, μηδὲ σὰ χιλιδόνι,
παρὰ ἐκελάϊδε κι ἔλεγε, ἀνθρωπινὴ λαλίτσα.
                    (Politis 1978:131)

It did not sing like a bird or like a swallow.
On the contrary, it sang and spoke with a human voice.

The metaphor of human beings as birds is the most prominent feature of the following funeral lament, which is also sung at weddings just before the departure of the bride from her home.

28

—Περδικούλα γιορντανάτα καὶ καμαρωτή,
πῶς κοιμᾶσαι αὐτοῦ στὰ πλάγια, στ' ἀρογκέντημα;
Δὲ φοβᾶσαι τὰ σαΐνια, τὸν ἀσταυραϊτό;
—Τὰ σαΐνια τά 'χω 'δέρφια, τὸν ἀσταυραϊτὸ πατέρα.

"My little partridge, beautiful and proud,
how can you sleep alone out on the mountainsides, out in the fields?
Aren't you afraid of the hawks and the vultures?"
"The hawks are my brothers; the vulture is my father."

In the context of a wedding, this song is a statement by the bride that she is about to leave her family of origin and become a member of a new family, her husband's family. The contrast between the bride (a small ground-dwelling partridge) and her affines (large, fearsome birds of prey) is vivid.[33] The singer is concerned that the bride will come to harm at the hands of her affines (who frequently, in Greek folk songs, poison the bride, and who are metaphorically associated with the earth, which "eats" people). In the context of a funeral, the partridge represents the deceased, who is about to be consumed by the earth.

Birds are metaphorical human beings. They are like humans, but they exist outside of human society. They live in the world of nature, not in the world of culture. Therefore they are not bound by the obligations or limitations imposed on people by their participation in society. The freedom birds enjoy from human social obligations is suggested in the following lament:

29

—Ἑλένη μ', σοῦ κλαῖνε τὰ πουλιά, σοῦ κλαῖν' τὰ χελιδόνια.
—Γιατί μοῦ κλαῖνε τὰ πουλιά, γιατί τὰ χελιδόνια;
Ἐγὼ δὲν τά 'χω τίποτα, ἐγὼ δὲν τά 'χω σόι.
Μένα μὲ κλαίει ἡ μάνα μου μὲ πόνο καὶ μὲ δάκρυα.
Μένα μὲ κλαῖν' τ' ἀδέρφια μου μὲ πόνο καὶ μὲ δάκρυα.

---

[33] The *saini*, the European sparrow hawk (*Accipiter nisus*), preys mainly on small birds, while the *stavraitos*, the bearded vulture (*Gypaëtus barbatus*), often attacks sheep and goats (Grzimek 1972, 7:362–363, 401–406).

"Eleni, the birds and the swallows are weeping for you."
"Why are the birds and the swallows weeping for me?
I'm not related to them. They are not my kin.
My mother is weeping for me with pain and with tears.
My brothers and sisters are weeping for me with pain and with tears."

Crying over the graves of her relatives is an obligation imposed upon a woman by virtue of her participation in a network of human social relationships. Birds, however, have no reason to cry, for they are not a part of this social network, just as foreign women have no obligation to wash a person's clothes or even to provide him with a proper burial.[34] It is this network of social relationships, the social context within which rural Greek death rites are performed, that is the subject of the next chapter.

IN THE RICH and moving tradition of Greek funeral laments marriage, *xenitia*, plants, food, water, poison, tears, and birds are all associated with the attempt to mediate the opposition between life and death, to move from an awareness of this opposition to its resolution. Each of these images attempts to provide a means of overcoming the contradiction between life and death, but this is an impossibility. The attempt is doomed to failure. But the movement from the extreme opposition between life and death through weaker oppositions is repeated again and again, until, as Lévi-Strauss (1967:226) has said, "the intellectual impulse which has produced it is exhausted."

Greek funeral laments, like all symbolic activity concerned with death, are extremely rich in metaphors of mediation because the process of dying and the body of the person who dies are mediators, par excellence, not only of the opposition between life and death but also of the opposition between nature and culture. Dying is the transition from life to death, from culture to nature. At death the human body passes from the world of the living to the world of the dead, from a cultural being to a natural object. These oppositions cannot be resolved. The contradictions inherent in our mortality cannot be overcome. The dead will never return.

---

[34] See lament 14.

115

5

WOUNDS THAT NEVER HEAL

THE RITES of passage associated with death and the singing of funeral laments occur within a particular social context that allows the bereaved to sustain a social relationship with the deceased. This relationship enables the living to carry on a "conversation" with the dead, a conversation through which the socially constructed world of the bereaved is maintained in spite of the threat presented by the death of the deceased.[1] This conversation, however, does not continue indefinitely. It draws to a close with the rite of exhumation, when the deceased is fully incorporated into the world of the dead. Over the course of the liminal

---

[1] On the lament as communicative event and the singer as mediator through whom the dead speak to the living, see Caraveli-Chaves (1980).

117

period following death, the religious perspective within which the conversation between the living and the dead is sustained is gradually replaced by a common-sense perspective in which the finality of death is accepted.

An analysis of the social context within which Greek death rituals take place involves consideration of several important themes in rural Greek life, including patterns of post-marital residence, inheritance, obligation, reciprocity, and the position of women. In Potamia, as in many areas of mainland Greece, residence after marriage is generally patrilocal (Friedl 1962:60–64, Campbell 1964:57, du Boulay 1974:20, and Danforth 1978:66). In other words, the newly married couple usually lives in an extended-family arrangement in the house of the groom's father. This situation may last several years, until the groom and his father are able to build a new house nearby for the young couple to live in. In the case of the youngest son in a family, who will inherit his father's house, this situation lasts until his parents' death. Often, though, the more wealthy families in a village are able to provide a son with a new house near his father's house when he marries.

Patterns of inheritance in Potamia are also similar to those reported for other parts of mainland Greece (Friedl 1962:48–64, Campbell 1964:188, du Boulay 1974:21).[2] Each child is entitled to receive an equal share of his parents' property. A daughter inherits her share in the form of a dowry, which she receives from her parents at the time of her marriage. A son receives his share at marriage or at a later time, when his father divides his estate, an event that may occur at the father's death or several years earlier. The older couple, the parents of the groom, usually retain a portion of their property for themselves until death, at which time it is inherited by the youngest son, who has lived with and cared for his parents during their old age.

The youngest son thus inherits his father's house as well as an extra share of his parents' estate. The people of Potamia explicitly credit this to the fact that he cared properly for his parents while they were alive. This inheritance also

---

[2] In the Cyclades (Hoffman 1976, Kenna 1976) and in the Dodecanese (Herzfeld 1980a) there are significant differences in patterns of inheritance which may well have an important effect on the manner in which obligations to the dead are carried out. On the relationship between patterns of inheritance and the performance of funeral rites in antiquity see Alexiou (1974:4–23).

entails the duty to perform the entire sequence of death rites—funeral, memorial services, and exhumation—after their death. In exchange for his extra share, the youngest son should provide for his parents in death as he did during their life. In such cases the youngest son is held officially responsible for all the expenses involved in performing the death rites of his parents. His brothers and sisters may offer to help in the preparations for these rites or to contribute to the distribution of food at the memorial services, but strictly speaking they are under no obligation to do so. If, on the other hand, the old couple lived by themselves during the last years of their lives and were not cared for exclusively by the youngest son, then the portion of their estate over which they retained control is distributed equally among all their children. In that case all the children share the cost of performing the death rites of their parents.

Although the youngest son, as the male head of a nuclear family, is officially responsible for the care of his elderly parents in life and in death, he is not the person who actually performs these duties. Given the sexual division of labor that exists in rural Greece, caring for other people in life (which involves feeding, washing, and keeping company), as well as caring for them in death (which involves the performance of all the appropriate death rites), is a task performed exclusively by women. It is the women of a family who actually fulfill the family's obligations to its dead.

When certain basic demographic facts are taken into consideration, the system of inheritance and the sexual division of labor outlined here produce a definite pattern in the social relationships that are involved in the performance of rural Greek death rituals. For a variety of reasons (including the obligation to perform military service and the ideal that sisters marry before brothers) men in rural Greece tend to marry at an older age than women do.[3] The result of this tendency, in conjunction with the fact that men in Greece, as elsewhere, have a shorter life expectancy than women (Allen 1976:172), is that wives regularly outlive their husbands. This general conclusion is supported by the fact that the village of Potamia contained a great many widows and very few widowers.

For these reasons the social relationships involved in the care of the dead

[3] Campbell (1964:82–84) reports that among the Sarakatsani shepherds of northwestern Greece men marry at about age thirty, whereas women marry in their mid-twenties.

tend to assume a characteristic pattern. Typically, a man dies before his wife. Regardless of whether the expenses for the death rites are the official responsibility of the youngest son or of all the children together, or whether they are paid for by the wife from her husband's estate, the wife of the deceased plays an important part in making the decisions concerning the laying out of the body, the quality and quantity of food to be distributed at the funeral and at the various memorial services, and the type of grave to be constructed over the body. The wife of the deceased is also responsible for the daily care of the grave from the date of death until the exhumation five years later. Of the ten married men who lay buried in the village graveyard of Potamia in July 1979, eight were survived by their wives. In seven of these eight cases the wives had built expensive marble graves to honor the memory of their husbands. They also visited their husbands' graves daily.[4]

Most women are widows when they die. Even if they are not, their husbands, as men, are not directly involved in planning and carrying out the arrangements for the death rites. Although the youngest son of a dead woman is officially responsible for paying the cost of his mother's death rites, it is his wife, the daughter-in-law of the deceased, who actually carries them out. Since a daughter-in-law is not bound to her mother-in-law by ties of blood (she is a *xeni*) and since the relationships between the two women are typically characterized by conflict (du Boulay 1974:18 and 155, Danforth 1978:197–202), it is not surprising that the death rites of women are less elaborate and less expensive than those of men or that daughters-in-law care less attentively for the graves of their mothers-in-law than wives care for the graves of their husbands.

Simple and inexpensive rectangular metal fencing marked the graves of six of the seven married women who lay buried in the graveyard of Potamia in July 1979. These six graves were visited relatively infrequently, perhaps once a week or less, by the daughters-in-law of the deceased women. The grave that was marked by a marble monument, on the other hand, was visited daily by the daughter-in-law of the woman who lay buried there. This daughter-in-law was singled out and complimented highly for the dedication with which she cared

---

[4] The one married man whose grave was not cared for by his wife was Kostas, whose situation was described in Chapter 1. His mother assumed responsibility for the performance of his death rites.

for her mother-in-law both in life and in death. Village women said that when she sat at the grave of her mother-in-law she would feel not only pain and sorrow at her mother-in-law's death but also pride and satisfaction at having fulfilled her obligations so faithfully.

The more common situation, in which a daughter-in-law fails to devote proper care and attention to the graves of her mother-in-law or father-in-law, is illustrated in the following account:

> Katerina and her husband lived alone, in spite of the fact that they had two married sons who had settled in Potamia. Before his death Katerina's husband had given five *stremata*[5] to each of his sons and had kept ten *stremata* for himself and his wife. When he died, Katerina paid all the expenses associated with his funeral and his memorial services. She visits his grave daily. Her two daughters-in-law contributed very little to the funeral meal. They did not even attend the forty-day memorial service in memory of their father-in-law, nor do they visit his grave. A few months after his death they stopped wearing black. Now Katerina's sons and her daughters-in-law complain that she spends too much money on candles and olive oil for her dead husband.
>
> Several months after her husband's death Katerina moved in with one of her sons, but when he demanded that she give him title to her ten *stremata* right then and there, she refused and moved out to live alone again. Katerina's two daughters-in-law are uniformly criticized by the women of Potamia for not showing more respect for their dead father-in-law. Women say disapprovingly: "They inherited so much property from him, and they can't even go light a candle for him." Katerina's sons are also criticized for not forcing their wives to show more respect for their father-in-law. In addition, both her sons and her daughters-in-law are critized for not taking better care of Katerina herself.

It is generally acknowledged that a person's daughters will care for him both in life and in death better than his daughters-in-law because his daughters are

---

[5] One *strema* (plural *stremata*) is a thousand square meters, approximately a quarter of an acre.

121

linked to him by blood ties, or, as one man said, "because they are my own offspring" (*yati ine sperma dhiko mou*).[6] As a result, daughters care for the grave of a dead parent because of the grief they feel at his death, whereas daughters-in-law care for the grave of a parent-in-law (if in fact they do so at all) out of a sense of social obligation, so that they will not be criticized by other women in the village. The behavior of Katerina's daughters-in-law contrasts sharply with the care that three sisters lavished on the grave of their father, a man who had no sons and thus no daughters-in-law. It is one of the structural contradictions of social life in rural areas of mainland Greece that because the youngest son resides in and inherits his parents home, it is their daughter-in-law who will care for them both in life and in death, and not their daughter, who would do so much more faithfully.

One further example will illustrate the typical pattern of social relationships brought into play at a person's death.

Kyriakos died in 1979. He was survived by his wife, two married sons, one married daughter, and many grandchildren. Many years earlier, when his oldest son Petros married a village woman named Panayota, the entire extended family lived and worked together for ten years until Petros and his father were able to build a new house nearby for Petros and his wife. During those ten years the income from the fields that constituted Panayota's dowry was used to cover the expenses of the entire extended family.

At about the time Petros and Panayota moved into their new house, Kyriakos' second son Nikos married Dhespina, and the young couple lived together with Kyriakos and his wife in the family home, which was completely renovated with money from Dhespina's dowry. Several years later Kyriakos' daughter and youngest child, Eleni, was married. Kyriakos gave her one quarter of his land as a dowry. At this time he also gave one quarter of his land to Petros and one quarter to Nikos. He

---

[6] *Dhikos*, referring to that which is one's own, that which is inside the reference group in question, is the term that contrasts with *xenos*, that which is foreign, other, or outside.

kept one quarter for himself and his wife. Shortly before his death Kyriakos left his remaining share to Nikos with whom Kyriakos and his wife would continue to live until their deaths. When Kyriakos died, Nikos was responsible for all the expenses incurred during the performance of his father's death rites.

Now Kyriakos' wife visits his grave daily. Since she and Dhespina live in the same household, and since one representative from a household is sufficient, Dhespina does not visit her father-in-law's grave. She is not criticized for her absence. It is understood that she will eventually be responsible for the care of her mother-in-law's grave. Kyriakos' daughter Eleni also visits her father's grave regularly, as does Panayota. The women of Potamia think highly of Panayota because, although she and her husband Petros received nothing for the ten years during which they contributed to the maintenance of the extended family (Kyriakos might have split the last share of his land evenly between Petros and Nikos), she does not complain and often comes to light a candle on her father-in-law's grave. This is the mark of a good daughter-in-law.

Proper performance of the entire sequence of death rites places a serious financial burden on a family. In Potamia the cost of these rites may run as high as two thousand dollars. The major expenses of the funeral are the casket, the digging of the grave, and the marble grave monument. At all death rites one must pay for the services of the priest, the food that is distributed, and the meals that are served. In addition, there is the cost of the olive oil and the candles that are burned at the grave of the deceased every day for five years. In order to emphasize how high these costs can be, villagers point out that it costs almost as much to care for a dead person during the first year after his death (when the bulk of the expenses occur) as it does to provide for a living person for the same period of time.

The women of Potamia are very interested in all the detailed arrangements involved in the performance of these rites, and they are aware of the amount of money each family spends in carrying them out. They are quick to praise elaborate and expensive preparations that properly honor the memory of the deceased, and even quicker to criticize arrangements that are judged to be inappropriately plain and simple. For example, after the funeral of a man who had no children of his own, his adopted daughter, who had been responsible for the funeral arrangements, was soundly criticized by many village women for having failed to celebrate his funeral more elaborately. She had not placed carpets in the room where the body lay prior to the funeral service; she had not ordered enough pastries or the proper kind of bread to distribute at the funeral; and she had tried to save money by putting very little olive oil in the rice that was served at the meal following the funeral. The general consensus was that the deceased had been the head of a very respectable household and that he had worked hard, raised his adopted daughter as his own child, and provided her with a substantial dowry. However, because she was not his own child, because she was ultimately a *xeni*, an unrelated person, she had not carried out his funeral in a sufficiently distinguished and dignified manner.

It is clear, then, that death rituals in rural Greece are public performances that are carefully evaluated in order to determine whether the living have properly fulfilled their obligations to the dead. The performance of these rites is often referred to as an obligation (*ipohreosi*) or as duties (*kathikonda*) owed the dead in return for the house and the property that the living inherit from them. The right to inherit entails the reciprocal obligation to perform death rituals. In this way the living and the dead, people of different generations, are linked together in a system of rights and obligations.

That the performance of these rites is a form of repayment for inheritance received is explicitly acknowledged by many Greek villagers. A woman of Potamia whose two brothers had emigrated to the United States defended the fact that she had inherited her parents' house (contrary to the usual practice by which the youngest son inherits the house) by saying that after her father's death she had performed all the necessary rites and that she was still caring faithfully for her elderly mother. This comment reveals the importance of the theme of mutual help or aid (*alilovoithia*), which plays such an important part in Greek culture (du Boulay 1974:142–168). The importance of the theme of reciprocity is indicated by the proverb "only mountains don't meet up with one another" (*vouno me vouno dhen andamonete*), which implies by contrast that people do meet up with one another. This proverb is usually used by a person who had just been thanked for helping another person. It says, in effect, "Don't mention it. Now you are obligated to me, but someday I'll need your help in return."

This relationship of reciprocity between members of adjacent generations is not only expressed in the rule that the youngest son, who cares for his elderly parents, inherits his father's house and an extra portion of his father's estate, and in return must pay for his parents' death rites. It is also expressed in rural Greek naming practices, according to which a child usually receives at baptism the name of a grandparent. As Herzfeld (1980b:2) points out, baptismal names are regularly conferred in response to some sort of social obligation. In Potamia and in other areas of mainland Greece where the youngest son inherits his father's house, a man honors his parents and repays them for that which he has inherited from them by conferring their names on his children. Thus naming children after parents is a way to fulfill one's obligations to one's parents, as is caring for their graves.

The performance of death rituals, in addition to being the fulfillment of a social obligation, is also an opportunity for the public expression of family solidarity. There is a general desire for these rites to be performed in an elaborate and impressive manner in order to uphold a family's reputation. On the other hand, if the performance of these rites is not judged appropriate and is found wanting in some respect, the lack of family solidarity is exposed and the family's reputation suffers accordingly.

It is clear, then, that in order for the rites of passage associated with death to be performed properly, all the reciprocal obligations between the living and the dead must be fulfilled. This can only happen if there are people nearby who are obligated to the deceased and will therefore perform these rites properly. As a widow of Potamia said, in reference to the conclusion of the burial service, when all those present at the grave toss a handful of earth into the coffin, "Everyone must have other people to throw a little earth [over him]" (*O kathenas prepi na ehi kosmo na rixi ena spiri homa*).

Pleas to die in a social context where death rituals will be properly performed are found in laments that describe the horrors of death in *xenitia*, a place where no one is obligated to perform the necessary rites.[7] The desirability of dying at

---

[7] See lament 14 and Chapter 4, note 17.

home in order to ensure that one's death will be properly mourned by one's family is conveyed by the following verses, which were incorporated into several laments sung at the funeral of an old man who is here addressed as father.

30
Πατέρα, νά 'χης μάνα, νά 'χης ἀδερφή,
νά 'χης καλὴ γυναίκα, νὰ σοῦ κλαίη κι αὐτή.

Father, may you have a mother, may you have a sister,
and may you have a good wife, to weep for you as well.

In the past it was said that if the relatives of the deceased failed to fulfill their social obligations by performing the necessary rites, the deceased would not be fully incorporated into the world of the dead and might return to the world of the living. According to Lawson (1910:375–376), the people who were thought most likely to become revenants were those who had not received proper burial, those who had met with a violent death, those who had died under a curse, those who had led particularly evil lives, and those over whose dead bodies a cat or other animal had passed (indicating that the corpse had not been watched over carefully between the time of death and the time of burial). Revenants were said to return to the world of the living to inflict harm on their close relatives. This is but another example, in negative form, of the reciprocity discussed above. Here the failure of the living to fulfill their obligations to the dead leads to a situation in which the dead fail in return to fulfill their obligation to withdraw completely from the world of the living.

The existence of a set of obligations that the living must perform for the dead from the time of death until the exhumation five years later indicates that during this liminal period the living continue to engage in a form of social relationship with the deceased, who remains a part of their social organization until the rites of secondary treatment are completed. The deceased continues to play the part of a significant other for those who mourn his death even though he is no longer alive. As Hertz himself noted:

The brute fact of physical death is not enough to consummate death in people's minds: the image of the recently deceased is still part of the

126

system of things of this world, and looses itself from them only gradually by a series of internal partings. We cannot bring ourselves to consider the deceased as dead straight away: he is too much part of our substance, we have put too much of ourselves into him, and participation in the same social life creates ties which are not to be severed in one day. The 'factual evidence' is assailed by a contrary flood of memories and images, of desires and hopes. The evidence imposes itself only gradually and it is not until the end of this prolonged conflict that we give in and believe in the separation as something real. (Hertz 1960:81–82)

THE SOCIAL RELATIONSHIP that continues to link the bereaved to the deceased is in effect a conversation between the living and the dead. The rites of passage and the funeral laments that have been analyzed in detail in the previous two chapters constitute the language or code through which this reality-sustaining conversation takes place.

The conversation temporarily overcomes the separation between this world and the other world, and through it the deceased is kept alive, at least in the sense that the living continue to interact with him after his death. The living carry on as if they accept the message that the conversation contains: that the opposition between life and death can be mediated.

All this is predicated upon the belief that the dead continue to exist as sentient beings who are somehow aware of the activities performed by the living on their behalf. Many women claim that, by the grace of God (hari theou), the souls of the dead are able to perceive the care and attention that women in mourning lavish upon them. They believe that the souls of the dead are pleased by this care and benefit from it. One widow said that when she is tending her husband's grave, she asks herself, "How can I please him?" She feels she is serving (exipireti) her husband and that she is giving him satisfaction (efharistisi) and relief (anakoufisi). When she lights a candle at his grave, for example, she feels that she has brought him a gift. If she fails to do so, she feels guilty; she has a weight on her conscience (varos sti sinidhisi). She said that when a woman performs an elaborate funeral for her husband, "she sends him off well fed and pleased" (ton dhiohni hortato ky efharistimeno). The distribution of food at memorial services and the proper care of the grave ensures that the deceased "will have everything [he needs] in front of him" (tha ta 'hi ola brosta tou). She concluded by saying that when she is involved in such activities she too feels pleased. She feels as if her husband were still with her.

At times the conversation between the living and the dead takes literal form, as the living address the dead directly, calling out to them by name. A particularly poignant example of this occurred after the death of an elderly man, as his body lay on a low bed in the formal reception room of his house. With many of his relatives and village women gathered around the corpse, the widow of the deceased reproached her dead husband bitterly: "Thanasi, what have you done to me? What have you done? You went to sleep, and you never woke up. You abandoned us. You crippled us. You cut off our hands."

Later in the afternoon several nieces arrived from a distant town and immediately fell to their knees and embraced their dead uncle. Between verses of the laments being sung by the women present, the nieces addressed him as follows:

Uncle, we are all here. What can we do for you? You used to gather us around you like your children. We all would have come—husbands and grandchildren too—if the taxi driver had let us. Wake up and talk to us for the last time, uncle. You won't be here for the wedding of Vassiliki [his ten-year-old granddaughter].

Uncle, uncle, we'll shout for you for three days if you want. Wake up, uncle. Wake up and hear the songs. This is the last time we'll see you. Uncle, what can we give you to take to Anna [their dead sister]?

These moving attempts to converse with the dead are an expression of the strong desire on the part of the living to continue to communicate with those who have recently died. This desire is also expressed in funeral laments that make use of the metaphors of death as marriage and death as departure for *xenitia*. These laments regularly take the form of an actual dialogue between the bride and her family or between the person who has departed for *xenitia* and his relatives. In other laments the living ask the dead about conditions in the underworld, and the dead reply. In all cases the dead are portrayed as if they were alive and able to communicate with the living.[8] Lament 10 projects the death that has

---

[8] Examples of laments that take the form of a dialogue between the living and the dead

already taken place into the future and represents the deceased and his relatives as engaged in a discussion of their impending separation. Many laments refer to the desire of the dead to communicate with the living. In lament 26 the deceased asks the living to speak to him and to cry for him. In lament 2, which deals with the rite of exhumation, Eleni asks her mother to come to her grave and "open a window" so that they may talk.

Some laments stress the inability of the deceased to communicate with the living. This point is made graphically in the following lament, sung at the exhumation of Eleni.

31

Στὰ πράσινα λειβάδια καὶ στὰ κίτρινα
μᾶς κλέψαν' τὴν 'Ελένη, μᾶς τὴν πῆρανε.
—Δὲ φώναξες, 'Ελένη μ', νὰ σὲ βγάλουμε.
—Πῶς νὰ φωνάξω, καὶ πῶς νὰ 'πηλογηθῶ;
Τὸ στόμα βουλωμένο, μαντήλι στὸ λαιμό,
κι αὐτὸς ὁ πικρο-Χάρος βαροῦσε κοντακιές.

In the green and golden meadows
they kidnapped Eleni. They stole her away from us.
"Eleni, you didn't cry out so that we could rescue you."
"How could I cry out? How could I answer your call?
My mouth was gagged. There was a kerchief around my neck.[9]
And that vicious Haros was raining blows down on me."

There are also laments in which a dead person enjoins the living to continue to mourn for him and not to forget him. In this way he is able to continue to play a part in the social relationships of the living even after his death. Other laments refer to letters, written on the wings of birds or with ink made from tears, that the deceased asks to be delivered to his family.[10]

---

are laments 7–11, 20, and 21. For a detailed discussion of the antiphonal structure of Greek funeral laments see Alexiou (1974:131–160).

[9] This is a reference to the strip of cloth used to bind shut the lower jaw of the deceased shortly after death.

[10] See Passow (1972:264) and Politis (1978:198).

The following lament sung at a funeral in Potamia forcefully expresses the desire of the deceased to continue his conversation with his living relatives. The deceased is portrayed as still alive, and he speaks in the first person.

32
Ἀπόψε δὲν κοιμήθηκα καὶ σήμερα νυστάζω,
γιατὶ πολὺ κουβέντιασα μὲ τὴν καλή μ' ἀγάπη,
κι ἀκόμα δὲν τὴ χόρτασα κι ἔχω καρδιὰ καμένη.

I did not sleep last night, and today I am tired,
because I talked for a long time with my good wife.
I have not yet had my fill of her company, and
    my heart has been burned.[11]

Death, which is anticipated here by the feeling of tiredness and the speaker's implicit recognition that he will never completely satisfy his desire for talking with his wife, will come (or, more correctly, has come) as a premature interruption of a conversation, a conversation that is the essence of social life itself.

The social relationships between the living and the dead, which are carried on through the performance of the rites of passage associated with death, are modeled in many ways on the social relationships that exist among the living. The manner in which the living interact with the dead is in effect an extension of the manner in which the living interact with each other. This can be clearly seen in the similarities that exist between the care given the living in everyday life and the care given the dead during the performance of death rites. Not only is the care similar, but the categories of people who provide it are similar as well.[12]

Both in life and in death mothers care for their children, wives care for their

[11] This lament can be greatly extended by the repetition of the last two lines with the substitution of other kin terms for "my wife."

[12] Compare Lévi-Strauss (1970:231): "the imagery with which a society pictures to itself the relations between the dead and the living can always be broken down in terms of an attempt to hide, embellish or justify, on the religious level, the relations prevailing, in that society among the living."

husbands, and daughters-in-law care for the elderly. The major component of this care is the preparation and serving of food. The feeding of others, as noted earlier, is an essential feature of social life in rural Greece and is the epitome of the expression of love and solidarity within the family. The importance of food is equally apparent in the relationship between the living and the dead, for the distribution of food is an important event at all rites associated with death. This food, which is actually consumed by the living, is believed to make its way into the other world where it benefits the dead directly. This belief is illustrated (as is the close relationship between marriage and death) by the following account.

> Paraskevi had eight children. When one of her daughters married and left home, Paraskevi was distraught. She was so upset that when she cooked meals for her children, she could not bring herself to prepare only seven plates of food. She continued to prepare eight plates of food, even though her daughter was no longer there. She would give her daughter's serving to a young girl, an orphan, who lived nearby. She felt comforted because she knew that her daughter's serving was being eaten. It was as if her own daughter were eating it herself.

Funeral laments also refer to the fact that the living provide food that has been requested by the dead. The following lament, sung at the funeral of an old man who had three grandchildren, emphasizes both the role of food in the expression of family solidarity among the living and the importance of food in maintaining social relationships with the dead.

33

Ἐψὲς πέρδικα τσάκωσα καὶ σήμερα τρυγόνα.
Κι ἔκατσα τὴ μαγείρεψα σ' ἀρχοντικὸ τραπέζι,
κι ἐκάλεσα τὸ σόϊ μου κι ὅλους τοὺς συγγενεῖς μου.
Ν-ὅλοι κινοῦσαν κι ἔρχονταν, ν-ὅλοι μὲ τὴν ἀράδα.
Πατέρας μου δὲ φάνηκε, δὲ φάνηκε νὰ ἔρθη.
Μᾶς εἶπαν πὼς ἀρρώστησε βαριὰ γιὰ νὰ πεθάνη.
Ζητάει νερὸ 'π' τὸν τόπο του καὶ μῆλ' ἀπ' τὴ μηλιά του,
ζητάει καὶ μοσχοστάφυλο ἀπ' τὴν κληματαριά του.

Σὰν τ' ἄκουσαν τὰ 'γγόνια του, τὰ τρία ἀράδ' ἀράδα,
τό 'να τοῦ πάει κρύο νερό, κι ἕνα τὸ σταφύλι,
ἡ τρίτη ἡ μικρότερη τοῦ πάει τ' ἀφράτο μῆλο.
—Σήκω, παππού, νὰ φᾶς, νὰ πιῆς, νὰ καλογιοματίσῃς.
Νὰ πιῆς νερὸ 'π' τὸν τόπο σου καὶ μῆλ' ἀπ' τὴ μηλιά σου,
καὶ τὸ μοσχοστάφυλο ἀπ' τὴν κληματαριά σου.

Yesterday I caught a partridge, and today a turtle dove.
I cooked them and served them at an elegant banquet.
I invited all my kin; I invited all my relatives.
Each of them set out and came, one after another.
Only my father failed to appear. Only he failed to come.
They told us that he had fallen ill and was about to die.
He called for water from his well and for an apple from his orchard.
He called for muscat grapes from his arbor.
When his grandchildren heard this, the three of them in turn,
one brought him cold water, another grapes.
The third, the youngest of them all, brought him a round red apple.
"Get up, grandfather! Eat! Drink! Have a good meal.
Drink water from your well. Eat an apple from your orchard,
and muscat grapes from your arbor."

In addition to providing food, mothers, wives, and daughters-in-law perform other services for the dead that they also perform for the living. Bereaved women provide the dead with water by crying and watering the flowers on their graves. During their daily visits to the graveyard they also wash, clean, and scrub the graves of the dead "as if they were houses."[13] At such times their activities bear a striking resemblance to the endless round of household tasks that fill the everyday lives of the village women of Greece. Bereaved women provide light for the dead ("so they can see, so they won't be in the dark") by lighting candles and olive oil lamps at the graves daily. They also feel that by sitting at the graves

[13] On water and washing see laments 14, 24, 25, and 26. On the grave as a home see Chapter 3, note 13.

for an hour or more everyday they are "keeping the dead company" (*kanoun parea me tous pethamenous*).

The parallel between the care provided the dead and that provided the living was explicitly recognized by a widow as she sat on the grave of her husband who had died just a few days earlier. She said: "Maria [the granddaughter of the deceased] will water the flowers on his grave every day. When he was alive, he used to ask her to bring him a glass of water." By caring for the dead as they care for the living the women of rural Greece are able to deny, symbolically and temporarily at least, the reality of death. They maintain social relationships with the dead through ritual and song in much the same way as they do with the living.

The site of this interaction, the place where the conversation between the living and the dead takes place, is the grave. A person's grave serves to maintain the reality of his existence in tangible form, in the world of physical space, for those who want to continue to engage in a social relationship with him. Not only is the grave a kind of house or home for the deceased, it is also a second house or second home (*dheftero spiti*) for the bereaved woman, who spends so much time there visiting and caring for her dead relative.[14] In addition a grave is often personified. It comes to stand for the deceased himself. A mother who has lost her child does not say, "I am going to my son's grave." She says, "I am going to my son" (*Tha pao sto pedhi mou*). Elderly widows at the graves of their husbands frequently say, "I'll wash the old man" (*Tha plino ton papou mou*), not "I'll wash the grave of the old man." As she left the graveyard every evening, one widow would pat the marble headstone of her husband's grave with her hand and say, "Until tomorrow, Nikos." Because of the personification of the grave, its destruction after the exhumation is a particularly powerful symbol of the finality of death and of the end of the social relationship that existed between the living and the dead during the liminal period.

Social relationships between the living and the dead are also maintained through the recitation of the names of the deceased. During church services on the *Psihosavata* (Soul Saturdays), which occur throughout the year, village priests

[14] Hirschon (1978:72) makes a similar point when she says that the graveyard is an "important focus of female activity, an extension of the domestic realm since concern is for maintenance of the grave, its cleanliness and attractive appearance." See also Hirschon (1980:9–11).

read the names of all those who have died in the village over the past few generations. Women are responsible for keeping lists of the names of their deceased relatives. These names are given to the village priest on *Psihosavata*, as well as at the performance of any *Trisayio* that occurs in the graveyard after a memorial service or on a Saturday evening after vespers. By reading the names of the village dead and by giving gifts to the church in their names, the living commemorate the dead.

The memory of the dead is also kept alive through the practice noted earlier of naming children after their grandparents. It is particularly important that this be done if the person whose name is to be given has died and no child has yet received his name. For example, in Potamia, as in many areas of Greece, the first son in a family regularly receives the name of his father's father. This is done "so that the name [of the grandfather] will not disappear, so that the name will be heard" (*na mi zvisi to onoma, n' akouyete to onoma*). When a man hears his son called by his father's name, he feels joy. When people hear the dead person's name applied to a young child, the deceased is remembered. He is brought back to life (*zondanevi*). It is as if the child were the dead person himself.

However, although this naming system links present and past generations and endows the deceased with renewed life, the "resurrection" is only temporary. As Herzfeld (1980b:6) has argued, "given the limited pool of available Christian names (see Bialor 1967) and their constant repetition, such short-term resurrection turns out to be a guarantee of total de-individuation in the long term. The systematic repetition of a name and its extension to an ever widening circle of descendants rob it in time of any association with its 'original' persona."

The sequence of short-term resurrection followed by long-term de-individuation that results from the naming system is identical to that brought about by the rite of exhumation. Over the short term, during the liminal period between death and exhumation, the deceased is kept alive, as it were, by means of the ritual performances of the living who care for his grave, just as he is when his name is given to his grandchild. The exhumation, like the conferral of the name, is an attempted resurrection. However, consignment of the bones of the deceased to the ossuary and the collective care of the community, like the repetition and extended application of the name of the deceased to more and more descendants, ensures ultimate oblivion. The naming system, then, like the rite of exhumation, involves only a partial and incomplete resurrection.

Social relationships between the living and the dead are also maintained through dreams. According to many people in Potamia, dreams represent the experiences of the immaterial portion of a human being. When someone dreams of a particular place, for example, his soul is thought to have traveled there. Similarly, when someone sees a dream in which he interacts with another person (alive or dead) or with one of the many saints of the Orthodox Church, it is thought that the souls of the two beings have come into contact.

Women in mourning frequently report dreams in which the soul of a dead person appears to them with a request that some service be performed. The deceased may ask for food, clothing, light, water, company, the exhumation of his remains, or simply not to be forgotten. Such dreams are taken as evidence for the continued existence of the soul after death and are believed to be messages from the deceased that are to be taken seriously and carried out as soon as possible. For example, the widow of a man who had been killed in World War II, and whose body had stiffened to the extent that pants were simply draped over the lower half of the corpse, had a dream in which her husband appeared to her and requested a belt because his pants would not stay up. She promptly bought a belt and gave it to a poor villager. Several days later her husband appeared to her in a second dream and thanked her for the belt. Satisfied, he did not disturb her sleep again.

Dreams, therefore, constitute a channel through which the dead are believed to be able to communicate with the living. When the requests made through dreams are fulfilled, the dead are believed to be satisfied and to have no more reason to contact the living. For that reason, and because the exhumation is the final obligation the living must perform for the deceased as an individual, people whose remains have been exhumed rarely appear to the living in dreams. This is further evidence that social relationships between the living and the dead are only temporarily maintained through the performance of death rituals, and that they gradually draw to a close at the end of the liminal period following death.

IT IS significant that the obligations to perform death rituals and sing laments, the very activities that constitute the conversation between the living and the dead, rest almost exclusively in the hands of women.[15] The only death ritual

[15] The only exception to this is the village priest, whose role is limited to the performance of the funeral service itself and to the reading of the *Trisayio* on various occasions during the rites of passage following death.

attended by men in large numbers is the funeral. Male members of the immediate family of the deceased attend the exhumation, as well as the more important memorial services forty days and one year after death. All other activities associated with death involve only women. Women prepare corpses for burial, lament, distribute food at memorial services, care daily for the graves of the dead, and exhume their remains. In addition, the restrictions imposed on women in mourning are much more severe than those imposed on men.

The contrast between the beliefs men and women hold concerning death is also striking. Men are much more likely to express skepticism concerning the continued existence of the soul after death and its ability to perceive or benefit from the services performed for it by women in mourning. Men often encourage their wives and other female relatives to devote less time and energy to the care of the deceased and to visit the graveyard less frequently, once a week, perhaps, instead of every day. Men argue that such intense involvement with the dead can only lead to increased grief and pain, which may in turn cause illness. The question remains, then: Why is it only women who participate in the social relationships that link the world of the living and the world of the dead?

The answer to this question lies in the respective positions that men and women occupy in rural Greek society.[16] In Greece, as in many areas throughout the world, women are denied the authority and prestige that men are accorded. This leads to an asymmetrical relationship in the cultural evaluation of the sexes (Rosaldo and Lamphere 1974:17). The concentration of residence and descent in the male line in most parts of mainland Greece contributes to the subordinate position of rural Greek women.

With the exception of the role of elementary-school teacher, all the prestigious public roles that exist in rural Greek society are open only to men. Male activities in general are believed to have higher prestige than female activities. Men and women also enjoy differential access to public space. Women are denied access to many public places that are open to men and must show deference to

---

[16] For a more thorough treatment of this important issue than is possible here see Campbell (1964:31–35, 263–304), Friedl (1967), du Boulay (1974:100–141 and passim), and Danforth (1978:70–82). On the position of women in Balkan societies in general see Denich (1974).

men on all public occasions. In short, men exercise culturally legitimated authority over women.

The marginal position of women in rural Greek society is indicated by the fact that "feminine roles are organized round a single element, that is to say the presence or the lack of a man. . . . Thus, socially as well as symbolically, a man is the vital validating factor of a woman's life" (du Boulay 1974:121). A woman's identity and her position in society is largely defined in terms of the men to whom she is related. Over the course of her life a woman moves from being someone's daughter to being someone's wife and someone's mother. The fact that women are identified in terms of the men to whom they are related is clearly demonstrated by several aspects of the Greek naming system that have not yet been discussed.

All children receive their father's surname, and at marriage a woman assumes the surname of her husband. Furthermore, a woman's surname is always given in the genitive (possessive) case.[17] It is common practice in Potamia and other parts of rural Greece to use, both as a term of reference and as a term of address, not the baptismal name of a married woman but the feminine form of her husband's baptismal name (Campbell 1964:186, Allen 1976:189). Thus Eleni, the wife of Yannis, is addressed and referred to as Yannena, and Maria the wife of Yorghos as Yorghena.

Although the important positions in the social structure of rural Greece are occupied by men, they are linked to one another through women. Women embody social ties. It is the woman who "is thought to hold the house together not only by her physical activity in making the place a sanctuary from the outside world in which food, warmth, and peace are to be found, but also by the ritual activities by which in a metaphysical sense she guards and protects her family" (du Boulay 1974:131). Campbell's observation (1964:168) that "the mother plays a role expressive of the solidarity of the family" supports the claim that it is primarily women in rural Greek society who maintain affective kin bonds.

Several comments by the women of Potamia also confirm this view. It is said that the tie between a woman and her children is stronger than that between a man and his children because there can never be any doubt as to who a child's

---

[17] See Hirschon (1978:87, note 5).

137

mother is, whereas there can often be doubt as to who a child's father is. A mother is also closer to her children than a father is because a father, like a guest or visitor (*mousafiris*), spends much of his time outside the home. One woman summed up the role of women in rural Greek society with her statement that a woman's whole life consists of being with her family. The lives of women in rural Greece, then, acquire meaning through the maintenance of social relationships with other members of their families.

It has often been observed that the more the bereaved defined themselves in terms of their relationship to the deceased, the more the death threatens their socially constructed world (Bynum 1973, Blauner 1977). Therefore it is not surprising that because of the marginal position of women in rural Greek society and because of the important part that the maintenance of social relationships plays in their lives, women are much more threatened by the death of a significant other than men are. Because a woman's identity depends greatly on her relationship to a man, the death of this man deprives her of the crucial component of her identity. At marriage a woman ceases defining herself in terms of her father and begins to define herself in terms of her husband; at the death of her husband a woman is left "without the essential factor she needs to validate her life" (du Boulay 1974:123).

For these reasons it is necessary for a woman, much more than it is for a man, to maintain the social relationships she enjoyed with the deceased. She must continue this relationship beyond the death of the significant other in order to prevent her sense of identity and her position in society from being overwhelmed. Through the performance of the elaborate sequence of death rites a woman is able to continue being a wife even after the death of her husband. She continues to visit him, to converse with him, to care for him, to feed him, even to wash and clean for him. Similarly, through the performance of these rites a woman continues to act as a mother even after the death of her child. In the last analysis, then, it is because of their marginal position in rural Greek society that women express so much more forcefully than men their belief that the souls of the dead benefit from their service. It is for this reason that women participate so much more fully than men in the performance of death rituals. They must do so in order to continue to be who they were prior to the deaths of the men who gave their lives definition and meaning.

By contrast, since a man does not define himself in terms of the women to whom he is related, the death of a woman does not pose a significant threat to his sense of identity or to his position in society. Therefore he does not need to maintain his relationship to her by observing a long period of mourning or by participating in the long sequence of death rituals.

THESE SOCIAL RELATIONSHIPS uniting the living and the dead, which are maintained by the women of rural Greece, exist in the context of what Clifford Geertz has called a religious perspective. The religious perspective "moves beyond the realities of everyday life to wider ones which correct and complete them." It rests on a "sense of the 'really real' . . . which the symbolic activities of religion as a cultural system are devoted to producing, intensifying, and so far as possible, rendering inviolable by the discordant revelations of secular experience" (Geertz 1973:112). It is in the context of this religious perspective, in the language of religious rituals and funeral laments, that the conversation between the living and the dead is carried on. Within this perspective the souls of the dead exist and have needs that are met by the daily visits of women to the graveyard. This is the reality generated by religious ritual and validated by religious belief.

The religious perspective on reality, which denies the finality of death and holds out the possibility of meaningful communication with the dead, can be maintained subjectively for a time by those in mourning. However, it is difficult to maintain this perspective in the face of the world of objective facts, "the discordant revelations of secular experience." The religious perspective is often contradicted by what Geertz calls a common-sense perspective, a perspective in which the paramount reality of human experience is that "everyday world of common-sense objects and practical acts . . . in which we are most solidly rooted, whose inherent actuality we can hardly question . . . and from whose pressures and requirements we can least escape" (Geertz 1973:119). In Hertz's terms "the 'factual evidence' is assailed by a contrary flood of memories and images, of desires and hopes" (1960:82). In a common-sense perspective, then, the finality of death is not denied in spite of the hope offered by religion. The contradiction between a religious and a common-sense perspective as far as death is concerned is the contradiction between the denial of death and its acceptance, the contradiction inherent in our mortality.

Paradoxically the religious perspective and the common-sense perspective, two "radically contrasting ways of looking at the world" (Geertz 1973:120), at times seem to be held jointly by the women of rural Greece, so rapidly do they move back and forth between them. This paradox is embodied in the ambivalent and contradictory attitudes that are so often associated with death in Greek culture. On one hand women express a fatalistic or realistic acceptance of death and the end to their relationship with the dead. On the other hand they express a conflicting desire for the continuation of this relationship, a hope that the dead can be kept alive, that they may even return.

The juxtaposition of these two conflicting perspectives is occasionally revealed in the comments of women in mourning as they discuss death and the death rituals that occupy so much of their time. For example, a woman trying to comfort a widow who was industriously sweeping the ground around the grave of her dead husband said, "Tonight your husband will sleep all tucked in and nicely cared for," but then she added sadly: "It's all useless. It's all for nothing." Occasionally women who are meticulously washing and scrubbing the marble graves of their dead relatives with sponges, rags, steel wool, knives, bars of soap, water, and detergent mutter bitterly to themselves: "We're wasting our time. We're not accomplishing anything at all." Such comments suggest that some women are aware of the futility of their actions at the very moment they are performing them. This same ambivalence was also expressed in the answers women offered to questions about the meaning of the distribution of food at memorial services. After explaining that food is distributed "so that the dead may eat," they sometimes asked cynically, "But do the dead really eat?", to which the answer was understood to be a resigned "no, of course not."

During the early portions of the long liminal period that lasts from the time of death until the exhumation, the attitudes of those in mourning tend to be dominated by the religious perspective discussed above, in spite of the occasional expression of an awareness of the contradictions between this religious perspective and the reality of death. As long as the religious perspective is subjectively maintained, a woman in mourning can continue to inhabit the socially constructed reality that existed prior to the death of the relevant significant other. She can continue to interact with the deceased; she can carry on a reality-sustaining conversation with him through the performance of death rituals in his memory.

With the passage of time, however, the religious perspective becomes increasingly more difficult to maintain. In the face of everyday reality and the objective facts of death, it gives way to a common-sense perspective in which the reality of death is accepted. This shift from a religious to a common-sense perspective brings about, by the time of the rite of exhumation, which concludes the liminal period, an end to the social relationships between the living and the dead. The conversation is concluded as a new social reality is constructed, one that does not include the significant other, who is now long dead and whose remains lie, largely forgotten, in the village ossuary in the corner of the graveyard.

In order to understand the manner in which the original social reality of the bereaved is maintained, and the process by which a new reality is constructed and death finally accepted, it is necessary to consider why women in mourning engage so intensely and for so long in their social relationships with the dead. The answer given most frequently by the bereaved women of Potamia as to why they visit the graveyard every day for five years is, "The pain pulls me" (*Me travai o ponos*). The concept of *ponos* (plural, *poni*), which can be glossed as pain, grief, suffering, or sorrow, is essential to an appreciation of the emotional experience of women in mourning in rural Greece. All the care and attention that women devote to their dead relatives is motivated by *ponos*, or *kamoudhia*, another term used in this context, which is a local variant of the standard term *kaimos*, meaning anguish, sorrow, yearning, or pained longing. Women go to the graveyard because they have *ponos*, because they have *kamoudhia*. Without these emotions, they say, they would not go anywhere. Even if women do not really want to go to the graveyard, the *ponos* they feel for the dead forces them to go. Women often say, "The *ponos* doesn't allow you not to go" (*O ponos dhe s'afini na min pas*).

The complex of emotions denoted by the term *ponos* is an expression of the social bonds that tie people together. One feels *ponos* at a person's death because one enjoyed close social relationships with him, and it is *ponos* that makes one want to continue this relationship after death. It is the *ponos* one feels at a person's death that makes one deny the finality of death and cling to the hope that death is, like the departure at marriage or the departure for *xenitia*, a departure from which a return is possible. In the words of one woman, "The *ponos* doesn't let you give up your hopes" (*O ponos dhe s'afini na kopsis tis elpidhes*).

It is this *ponos*, then, that maintains the religious perspective toward death and enables the conversation with the deceased to continue. It is this *ponos* that prevents the full acceptance of death and leads those in mourning to believe that a return from the world of the dead is possible. Because of this complex of emotions a situation devoid of hope is transformed into a situation with hope. People are led to take literally, for a time at least, the metaphors of death as marriage and death as *xenitia*. *Ponos* makes one treat the deceased as if he were still alive. If a woman feels *ponos* and *kamoudhia*, then she will deny that the time and the money she spends caring for the grave of the deceased are in vain. By creating hope, these emotions also change one's perceptions of the world. For example, people repeatedly told a woman who had spent a great deal of money on a very elaborate funeral for her eighty-year-old father that since he had been so old she should not have spent so much money. Invariably she replied: "He may have seemed old to you, but to me, because of the *ponos* I feel, he was not old."[18]

Because *ponos* generates hope, it also creates, somewhat paradoxically perhaps, a feeling of comfort and solace (*parighoria*), as well as a feeling of relief. It gives a woman the courage and the fortitude to continue caring for the grave of the deceased long after his death. In this sense, then, *ponos* is a desirable emotion. It is a positive expression of an emotional tie to another person. As one woman said:

> *Ponos* is necessary. It needs to be cultivated. Because I feel *ponos* for you and you feel *ponos* for me, we are comforted. A woman wants to feel *ponos* in order to find solace. I like to go to funerals and cry. I want to go because there I feel *ponos*. There I remember my own dead relatives. I feel sad then because I had parents too.

The following lament precisely captures this attitude toward *ponos*:

34
Ποῦ πᾶς, γαϊτάνι, νὰ σαπῆς, γκόλφι μου, ν' ἀραχνιάσης,
γαρούφαλο βενέτικο, ν' ἀλλαξομουσουδιάσης;

---

[18] In this case the daughter of the deceased was responsible for arranging his funeral since his wife had already died and since he had no sons and therefore no daughters-in-law.

Παιδάκι μου, τὸν πόνο σου ποῦ νὰ τὸν ἀπιθώσω;
Νὰν τόνε ϱίξω τϱίστϱατα, τὸν παίϱνουν οἱ διαβάτες,
νὰν τόνε ϱίξω στὰ κλαϱιά, τὸν παίϱνουν τὰ πουλάκια.
Θὰ τόνε βάλω στὴν καϱδιά, νὰν τὸν καταϱιζώσω,
νὰ πεϱπατῶ, νὰ μὲ πονῇ, νὰ στέκω, νὰ μὲ σφάζη.
Θὰν πάγω καὶ στὸ χϱυσικό, γιὰ νάν τονε χϱυσώση,
νὰ φκιάσω 'να χϱυσὸ σταυϱὸ κι ἕν' ἀσημένιο γκόλφι,
νὰ πϱοσκυνάγω τὸ σταυϱὸ καὶ νὰ φιλῶ τὸ γκόλφι.

(Petropoulos 1959:235)

How can a ribbon rot? How can an amulet get covered with cobwebs?
How can a precious carnation from Venice wither and die?
My child, where can I put the *ponos* I feel for you?
If I toss it by the roadside, those who pass by will take it.
If I throw it in a tree, the little birds will take it.
I will place it in my heart so that it will take root there,
so that it will cause me *ponos* as I walk, so that it will kill me as I
    stand.
I will go to a goldsmith to have it gold-plated.
I will have it made into a golden cross, into a silver amulet,
so that I can worship the cross and kiss the amulet.

Here the bereaved mother expresses the view that she must not allow the *ponos* she feels at the death of her child to dissipate. She must nourish her pain, her grief, her sorrow, as long as possible. She must cherish these emotions dearly because it is through them alone that she is able to keep alive the memory of her child.

It is inevitable, however, that over the course of the five-year liminal period the pain subsides, the conversation with the deceased draws to a close, and a new social reality is constructed which enables the bereaved to inhabit more fully a world in which the deceased plays no part. During this time bereaved women gradually adopt a common-sense perspective toward death, as the desire for continued interaction with the deceased and the hope for his return are crushed under the weight of the reality of death.

This process is brought about through a gradual reduction in the intensity of the emotions associated with death, through the formation of new social relationships with new significant others, and through the constant confrontation with the objective facts of death, climaxing in the exhumation of the bones of the deceased. The result of this process is as complete an acceptance of the final and irreversible nature of death as is possible.

Since the conversation between the living and the dead is continued because of the *ponos* experienced by those in mourning, this complex of emotions must somehow be dealt with in order for the conversation to end and a new conversation with new significant others to begin. Many Greek villagers subscribe to what can be called an indigenous theory of catharsis.[19] They recognize that in spite of the desirability of immersing oneself fully in the emotions of pain, grief, and sorrow, the ultimate goal of a woman in mourning is to rid herself of these emotions through their repeated expression.

It is generally accepted that a prolonged containment of such emotions can cause serious illness, both physical and psychological. For example, one woman said that after her father's death she had such a "fire" inside her that whenever she visited his grave she wanted to dig him up and hold him in her arms. She was so distraught that several women who lived nearby prevented her from visiting her father's grave for many days. During this time she developed a high fever, and boils broke out all over her body. People said that her skin disorder was a sign that "the evil had come out from inside" (*to kako vyike apo mesa*). They also felt that if she had been allowed to go to the grave and cry and sing laments she would not have fallen ill. With crying and singing, a knot (*komvos*) leaves one's throat, one is lightened (*elafreni*), and one feels cool (*dhrosizete*). When a woman visits the graveyard and cries, *ponos*, anxiety, and poison all leave her system. A woman performs the necessary rites of passage and cares for the graves of the dead "in order to get everything out of her system" (*ya na xespasi*). These visits to the graveyard are one of the few opportunities for the cathartic outburst of emotion (*xespasma*) available to a woman in mourning. There she may even sit and cry about private personal or family problems that are not

---

[19] Many anthropologists interested in ritual systems of psychotherapy have stressed the therapeutic functions of cathartic experiences. See, for example, Wallace (1959), Crapanzano (1973:222), Young (1975:568), and Danforth (1978:312ff.).

necessarily related in any way to death, but which cannot be shared with anyone or expressed in any other context.

Women not only feel more *ponos* than men at the death of significant others, but they also have fewer opportunities to express it, given the very restricted lives they lead. A man may go out in the evening to the village coffeehouse to drink and talk. A woman, however, is confined more closely to her home and yard. It is the confinement of women, and of women in mourning in particular, that renders the cathartic expression of contained emotion more difficult for them than for men.[20] The difference between men and women with regard to confinement, and the impact this difference has on their ability to express pain and grief, is conveyed in the following couplet:

35

Ἐσύ 'σαι ἄντρας, περπατᾶς, κι οἱ πόνοι διαβαίνουν.
Ἐγὼ γυναίκα, κάθομαι, κι οἱ πόνοι ἀναβαίνουν.

You are a man. You walk, and the *poni* pass.
But I am a woman. I sit, and the *poni* mount.

Women in mourning generally feel that it is preferable to have others with whom they can share these emotions. They agree, though, that only relatives can be trusted with such a private matter as the expression of grief. As a widow said in a lament she sang over her husband's grave, "Would that I had a brother in my neighborhood and sisters nearby so that I could tell them my *ponos*." However, because the people with whom one shares these emotions are relatives, they too will experience grief upon learning of death. The predicament generated by these contradictory feelings and the difficulty of finding someone with whom to share one's grief is captured in the following lament:

[20] Note the parallel between this catharsis and the "emergence" of widows from the confinement of mourning. Widows, like the bones of the deceased, "emerge" at the rite of exhumation, the very rite that brings to completion the therapeutic process of mourning itself.

145

36

Ποῦ νὰ τὸ πῶ τὸν πόνο μου, ποῦ νὰ τὸ 'μολογήσω;
Γιὰ νὰ τὸ πῶ στὴ γειτονιά, νὰ μὴν τὸ μάθ' ὁ κόσμος.
Γιὰ νὰ τὸ πῶ στὴ μάνα μου, δὲ θέλ' νὰ τὴ πικράνω.
Γιὰ νὰ τὸ πῶ στ' ἀδέρφια μου, δὲ θέλ' νὰ τὰ πικράνω.
Γιὰ νὰ τὸ πῶ καὶ στὰ παιδιά μ', δὲ θέλ' νὰ τὰ πικράνω.

Who can I talk about my *ponos* with? Who can I confess my *ponos* to?
If I talk about it with my neighbors, then the whole world will learn
    of it.
If I talk about it with my mother, I will cause her bitterness and grief.
If I talk about it with my brothers and sisters, I will cause them
    bitterness and grief also.
And if I talk about it with my children, I will cause them too
    bitterness and grief.

Another couplet, which refers specifically to the singing of funeral laments, conveys both the desirability of expressing one's feelings of pain as well as the difficulty of doing so.

37

Τὰ τραγούδια λόγια εἶναι, τὰ λέν' οἱ πικραμένοι.
Τὰ λέν' νὰ βγάλουν τὸ πικρό, μὰ τὸ πικρὸ δὲ βγαίνει.

Songs are just words. Those who are bitter sing them.
They sing them to get rid of their bitterness, but the
    bitterness doesn't go away.

As a widow of Potamia said, the ultimate goal of a woman in mourning is "to get rid of her *ponos*" (*na rixi ton pono exo*). She added, though, that in her case, and in the cases of many other bereaved women, this would never happen. They would die with their *ponos*. Then she compared her *ponos* to a wound, a wound that would never heal.

146

DURING her long period of mourning a woman's relationship to her deceased relative grows more and more attenuated. At the same time she forms new social relationships with new significant others. Given the restrictions imposed upon a woman in mourning, many of these new relationships are formed with other women in mourning.

The bereaved women of Potamia spend over an hour together every evening. For many of these women this is one of the few opportunities they have to leave their house and yard and talk with other women. As they sit at the graves they talk casually about everyday matters: their family, their crops, their household chores. They also discuss death in general, as well as the particular deaths that have touched them and their emotional responses to these deaths. They share their grief. Several women were said to have become close friends this way. They had become neighbors in a way, since the graves of their children were next to each other.

The interaction between women whose grief is still very intense and whose relationship to the deceased is still very close, on one hand, and women whose grief has been mitigated by the passage of time, on the other, is instructive. Those in the former category tend to be women whose relatives have died very recently or very tragically: a mother who has lost a child, or a young woman who has lost her husband after only a few years of marriage. The latter category is composed of women whose experiences with death have been less recent and less tragic: a woman whose mother or father died at a very advanced age three or four years earlier, for example. Women whose grief is less intense are much more likely to adopt a common-sense perspective toward death than are other women. They are therefore in a position to comfort women whose grief is more intense and to assist them in dealing with their pain and their hope, in shifting from a religious to a common-sense perspective, and in constructing a new social reality.

Women whose involvement with death is less threatening encourage other women to abandon their religious perspective toward death and to adopt a common-sense perspective. They do this by discouraging overly elaborate and excessive displays of grief and by pointing out gently but persistently that all efforts on behalf of the deceased are in vain, that the marble graves built by women who are experiencing intense grief are a waste of money, and that the hopes they have are all false. Women whose grief has faded try to comfort other women by pointing out to them still other women whose situations are even more tragic than theirs. All this is part of an explicitly recognized attempt to give women whose grief is still very intense the courage to put aside their hopes, to end their relationship with the deceased, and to accept the reality of death.

In the lives of women in mourning in rural Greece there is a constant tension between the religious and the common-sense perspectives toward death, a continuous struggle over which of the two will prevail. This struggle is played out every evening at the graveyard as the women whose grief is least intense get up from the graves, cross themselves, and prepare to leave. The other women, who are more involved in their relationship with the deceased, are not ready to leave. They do not want to bring their evening "conversation" with the dead to an end just yet. They are still sobbing and crying; they have just a little more scrubbing and cleaning to do. They want to wait just a little longer, until the candles burn out. The women who are ready to go will not leave the few remaining women to grieve alone. They try to convince them to leave, saying:

> Even if we sit here longer, we'll still have to leave sometime. If we stay here all night, the dead still won't rise from their graves. We can't do anything more. This is our fate. Come on. Let's go. It's late.

Another example of the difference between the attitudes toward the dead generated by these two perspectives involves a conversation that took place at the grave of a man who had died just six days earlier. His widow sat by the grave supporting herself with her hand, which rested on the freshly dug earth of his grave. Another widow, whose husband had died three months earlier, reprimanded her, saying: "Get off the grave. Why give him any more weight than he already has?" A third woman, whose mother-in-law had died several years earlier, quickly shot back: "Don't be silly. It doesn't matter. He's dead. He doesn't feel anything at all."

In this way, as a woman's pain and hope slowly fade, she enters into new relationships with people who have come a long way toward accepting death. These new conversations with new significant others gradually take the place of the conversation with the deceased, a conversation sustained, as time passes, with greater and greater difficulty. One of the most important reasons this conversation loses intensity, and thus one of the reasons a religious perspective toward death is gradually replaced by a common-sense perspective, is that the performance of the necessary death rituals forces women in mourning to confront continually the objective reality of death. Every day for five years the bereaved women of Potamia visit the graves of their dead relatives. Every day they are presented with visible evidence that their relatives have died and have been buried in the earth, never again to return to the world of the living. This daily confrontation forces upon these women the realization that the separation of death is final.

The shift from a religious perspective toward death to a common-sense perspective, which takes place gradually over the five-year period between death and exhumation, also takes place repeatedly, day after day, over the much shorter period of time between the daily journey of the women of Potamia to the graveyard and their return home about an hour later. This transformation of pain and hope into a resigned acceptance of death is apparent in the accounts offered by these women of their feelings on their way to and from the graveyard. Consistently the bereaved women of Potamia report that when they set out from their homes in the early evening they feel a kind of eagerness. They want to reach the grave quickly because they feel that they will see the deceased and that they will please him by talking to him and keeping him company. When they actually see the grave, though, they realize that the deceased is in fact dead, and the full impact of the death is driven home once more. This is the nadir of their emotional experience. They can only bring themselves to leave the graveyard with great difficulty. They think about the deceased and say to themselves: "Where did I leave him? I left him in the black earth." On their way back to their homes they feel exhausted, worn out, and bitter (*maramenes, komenes, pikramenes*). One woman compared these visits to the graveyard with the experience of going eagerly to the village store to talk by telephone with her children in the United States. After these conversations her excitement and anticipation were transformed into sadness and pain, because she realized even more fully than before how far away her children really were.[21]

[21] This example underscores the analogy between *xenitia* and death discussed in Chapter 4.

149

It is the rite of exhumation that ultimately forces bereaved women to accept the finality and irreversibility of death. The exhumation, which holds out the hope of bringing about a return of the deceased from the underworld, is in fact the final cruel step in a permanent departure. The rite of exhumation involves a destruction of the grave, which had been for so long a home to both the deceased and his bereaved relatives. The social relationships and the daily conversations that linked the living and the dead come to an end. At the exhumation the dead cease to exist as individuals: their dry, white bones are consigned to a collective existence in the village ossuary.

In contrast to all the attempts to mediate the opposition between life and death, in contrast to all the images of life and hope that are found in Greek funeral laments, there are also passages that grimly acknowledge the irreversibility of death.

> 38
> —Νὰ ἤξερα πότε θὰ 'ρθῆς ἀπὸ τὸν Κάτου κόσμο,
> νὰ κάμω γιόμα νὰ γευτῆς καὶ δεῖπνο νὰ δειπνήσης,
> νὰ πλύνω καὶ τὰ ροῦχα σου, νὰ 'ρθῆς νὰ τὰ φορέσης.
> —Ἄν κάμης γιόμα, γιέψου το, κι ἂν κάμης δεῖπνο, δεῖπνα,
> κι ἂν πλύνης καὶ τὰ ροῦχα μου, βάλε φωτιὰ καὶ κάφ' τα,
> τὶ ἐγὼ πίσω δὲν ἔρχουμαι καὶ πίσω δὲ γυρίζω.
> Πάου στῆς Ἄρνης τὰ βουνά, στῆς Ἄρνησας τοὺς κάμπους,
> 'π' ἀρνιέται ἡ μάνα τὸ παιδὶ καὶ τὸ παιδὶ τὴ μάνα,
> 'π' ἀρνιῶνται καὶ τ' ἀντρόγενα, τὰ πολυαγαπημένα.
>   (Petropoulos 1959:223)

"If I knew when you were returning from the underworld,
I would prepare a meal so you could eat, a dinner so you could dine,
and I would wash your clothes so you could wear them when you
    arrive."
"If you prepare a meal, you will eat it yourself. If you prepare a
    dinner, you will dine alone,
and if you wash my clothes, you should light a fire and burn them.
I am never coming back. I am never returning.

I am going to the mountains and fields of the Land of Denial,
where a mother denies her child, where a child denies its mother,
and where husbands and wives deny each other, even though they are
   very much in love."

39
—Ὡς πότε νὰ σὲ καρτερῶ καὶ νὰ σὲ παντυχαίνω;
—Ὥσπου νὰ στίξη ἡ θάλασσα, νὰ γίνη περιβόλι,
ὥσπου ν' ἀσπρίση ὁ κόρακας, νὰ γένη περιστέρι,
τότε καὶ σὺ καρτέρι με, τότε παντύχαινέ με.
                    (Petropoulos 1959:223)

"When should I expect you? Until when should I wait for you?"
"Until the sea runs dry and becomes a garden,
until the crow turns white and becomes a dove.
Expect me then. Wait for me until then."

In the first two lines of lament 38 the woman who is singing expresses her
hope that the deceased will return from the land of the dead through her offer to
care for him by cooking his meals and washing his clothes.[22] This hope is cruelly
shattered by the announcement of the deceased that he no longer needs these
services and that he will never return. The reference to the world of the dead as
the "Land of Denial" emphasizes the fact that death leads to an irreparable break
in social relationships.

Lament 39 expresses the absolute finality of death by means of a convention
known as the *adynaton*, meaning "the impossible." This convention, which is
put to powerful use in Greek funeral laments, involves the equation of a natural
or physical impossibility with an impossibility in the mind of the person who
employs the *adynaton*.[23] In this lament the impossibility of a return from life to
death is compared to the impossible transformation of the sea into a fertile garden

---

[22] On the importance of washing clothes and providing food in the maintenance of social
relationships see laments 14, 25, and 33.

[23] For this definition and for further discussion of the *adynaton* in Greek tradition see
Tuffin (1972–1973).

151

and the equally impossible transformation of a black crow into a white dove. The assertion by the deceased of the ultimate finality of death forcefully conveys to the living the futility of trying to continue any social relationship with those who have died. The conversation between the living and the dead, carried on through the performance of death rituals and the singing of laments, must come to an end. The dead will not return. They will not return "until the crow turns white and becomes a dove."

The death rituals and the funeral laments of rural Greece, then, are a symbolic language through which the bereaved women who perform them try to resolve the contradictions between life and death that are inherent in human mortality. They explore, through some of the most powerful symbols and metaphors of Greek culture, the possibility that the opposition between life and death might be mediated, that in the end death might be overcome. The performance of these rituals and the singing of these laments constitute, therefore, an admission that human existence is marred by an insurmountable contradiction that cannot be ignored. Death will continue to tear apart the socially constructed world of the women of rural Greece. Their parents, their husbands, and their children will continue to die. These new deaths will remind them of past deaths, call forth old pain, and reopen wounds that never fully heal.

BIBLIOGRAPHY

Alexiou, Margaret

    1974   *The Ritual Lament in Greek Tradition*. Cambridge: At the University Press.

    1978   Modern Greek Folklore and its Relation to the Past: The Evolution of Charos in Greek Tradition. In *Proceedings of the 1975 Symposium of Modern Greek Studies*, pp. 211–226. Berkeley: University of California Press.

    1980   Sons, Wives, and Mothers: Reality and Fantasy in Some Modern Greek Ballads. Paper delivered at the 1980 Symposium of the Modern Greek Studies Association. Philadelphia.

Alexiou, Margaret, and Peter Dronke

    1971   The Lament of Jephtha's Daughter: Themes, Traditions, Originality. *Studi medievali* 12(2):819–863.

Allen, Peter

    1976   Aspida: A Depopulated Maniat Community. In *Regional Variation in Modern Greece and Cyprus: Toward a Perspective on the Ethnography of Greece*, ed. M. Dimen and E. Friedl, 268:168–198. New York: Annals of the New York Academy of Sciences.

Basso, Keith

    1976   'Wise Words' of the Western Apache: Metaphor and Semantic Theory. In *Meaning in Anthropology*, ed. K. Basso and H. Selby, pp. 93–121. Albuquerque: University of New Mexico Press.

Beaton, Roderick

    1980   *Folk Poetry of Modern Greece.* Cambridge: At the University Press.

Berger, Peter

    1969   *The Sacred Canopy.* New York: Anchor Books.

Berger, Peter, and Hansfried Kellner

    1964   Marriage and the Construction of Reality. *Diogenes* 46:1–24.

Berger, Peter, and Thomas Luckmann

    1967   *The Social Construction of Reality.* New York: Anchor Books.

Bialor, Perry

    1967   What's in a Name? Aspects of the Social Organization of a Greek Farming Community Related to Naming Customs. In *Essays in Balkan Ethnology*, ed. W. G. Lockwood, pp. 95–108. Berkeley: Kroeber Anthropological Society Special Publication No. 1.

Blauner, Robert

    1977   Death and Social Structure. In *Passing*, ed. Charles O. Jackson, pp. 174–209. London: Greenwood Press.

Blum, Richard, and Eva Blum

    1970   *The Dangerous Hour: The Lore of Crisis and Mystery in Rural Greece.* New York: Charles Scribner's Sons.

Burke, Kenneth

    1954   *Permanence and Change: An Anatomy of Purpose.* Indianapolis: Bobbs-Merrill.

1964   *Perspectives by Incongruity.* Ed. Stanley Hyman. Bloomington: Indiana University Press.

Bynum, Jack
1973   Social Status and Rites of Passage: The Social Context of Death. *Omega* 4:323–332.

Campbell, John K.
1964   *Honour, Family and Patronage.* Oxford: Clarendon Press.

Caraveli-Chaves, Anna
1980   Bridge Between Worlds: The Greek Women's Lament as Communicative Event. *Journal of American Folklore* 93:129–157.

Crapanzano, Vincent
1973   *The Hamadsha: A Study in Moroccan Ethnopsychiatry.* Berkeley: University of California Press.

1980   Rite of Return: Circumcision in Morocco. In *The Psychoanalytic Study of Society*, vol. 9, ed. W. Muensterberger and L. B. Boyer. New York: Library of Psychological Anthropology.

Crick, Malcolm
1976   *Explorations in Language and Meaning: Towards a Semantic Anthropology.* London: Malaby Press.

Danforth, Loring
1978   *The Anastenaria: A Study in Greek Ritual Therapy.* Ph.D. dissertation, Princeton University. Ann Arbor, Mich.: University Microfilms.

1979   The Role of Dance in the Ritual Therapy of the Anastenaria. *Byzantine and Modern Greek Studies* 5:141–163.

Denich, Bette
1974   Sex and Power in the Balkans. In *Woman, Culture, and Society*, ed. M. Rosaldo and L. Lamphere, pp. 243–262. Stanford, Calif.: Stanford University Press.

du Boulay, Juliet
1974   *Portrait of a Greek Mountain Village.* Oxford: Clarendon Press.

Durkheim, Émile
1965   *The Elementary Forms of the Religious Life.* New York: Free Press. (1st French ed. 1912.)

Eco, Umberto
1979   *The Role of the Reader: Explorations in the Semiotics of Texts.* Advances in Semiotics. Bloomington: Indiana University Press.
Fabian, Johannes
1973   How Others Die—Reflections on the Anthropology of Death. In *Death in American Experience*, ed. A. Mack, pp. 177–201. New York: Schocken Books.
Farantou, Ch.
1975   Ta nekrotapheia kai ta nekrika ethima tis periohis Kavo Doro tis Euboias: Amygdalia. *Archeion Euboikon Meleton* 20:94–123.
Felouki, Evaggelia
1929   Nekrika ethima apo tin Alexandroupoli. *Laographia* 10:459–463.
Fernandez, James
1971   Persuasions and Performances: Of the Beast in Every Body . . . and the Metaphors of Every Man. In *Myth, Symbol, and Culture*, ed. C. Geertz, pp. 39–60. New York: W. W. Norton & Co.
1974   The Mission of Metaphor in Expressive Culture. *Current Anthropology* 15(2):119–145.
Frazer, James G.
1913   *The Belief in Immortality and the Worship of the Dead.* London:
–1924   MacMillan. (Vol. I, 1913; vol. II, 1922; vol. III, 1924.)
Friedl, Ernestine
1962   *Vasilika: A Village in Modern Greece.* New York: Holt, Rinehart and Winston.
1963   Some Aspects of Dowry and Inheritance in Boeotia. In *Mediterranean Countrymen: Essays in the Social Anthropology of the Mediterranean*, ed. J. Pitt-Rivers, pp. 113–135. Paris: Mouton.
1967   The Position of Women: Appearance and Reality. *Anthropological Quarterly* 40:97–108.
Geertz, Clifford
1973   *The Interpretation of Cultures.* New York: Basic Books.
Goody, Jack
1962   *Death, Property and the Ancestors: A Study of the Mortuary Customs of the LoDagaa of West Africa.* Stanford, Calif.: Stanford University Press.

BIBLIOGRAPHY

Grzimek, Bernhard

    1972   *Grzimek's Animal Life Encyclopedia*. New York: Van Nostrand Reinhold Co.

Hertz, Robert

    1960   A Contribution to the Study of the Collective Representation of Death. In *Death and the Right Hand*, pp. 27–86. Glencoe, Ill.: Free Press. (1st French ed. 1907.)

Herzfeld, Michael

    1977   Ritual and Textual Structures: The Advent of Spring in Rural Greece. In *Text and Context: The Social Anthropology of Tradition*, ed. R. Jain, A.S.A. Essays, 2:29–50. Philadelphia: Institute for the Study of Human Issues.

    1979   Exploring a Metaphor of Exposure. *Journal of American Folklore* 92:285–301.

    1980a   Social Tension and Inheritance by Lot in Three Greek Villages. *Anthropological Quarterly* 53:91–100.

    1980b   Norms, Exceptions, and Formal Properties: Some Baptismal Naming Systems of Rural Greece. Paper presented at the Annual Spring Meeting of the American Ethnological Society. Ann Arbor, Mich.

    1981a   Performative Categories and Symbols of Passage in Rural Greece. *Journal of American Folklore* 94:44–57.

    1981b   An Indigenous Theory of Meaning and its Elicitation in Performative Context. *Semiotica* 34:113–141.

Hirschon, Renée

    1978   Open Body/Closed Space: The Transformation of Female Sexuality. In *Defining Females*, ed. Shirley Ardener, pp. 66–88. New York: John Wiley & Sons.

    1980   The Opposition and Complementarity of Religious Life. Paper delivered at the 1980 Symposium of the Modern Greek Studies Association. Philadelphia.

Hoffman, Susannah

    1976   The Ethnography of the Islands: Thera. In *Regional Variation in Modern Greece and Cyprus: Toward a Perspective on the Ethnography of Greece*, ed. M. Dimen and E. Friedl, 268:328–340. New York: Annals of the New York Academy of Sciences.

Huntington, Richard, and Peter Metcalf
    1979 *Celebrations of Death*. Cambridge: At the University Press.
Ioannou, Giorgos
    1970 *To dimotiko tragoudi: Paraloges*. Athens: Ermis.
Kenna, Margaret
    1976 Houses, Fields, and Graves: Property and Ritual Obligation on a Greek Island. *Ethnology* 15:21–34.
Kosmas, Nikos
    1960 Ta moirologia ton Pramanton. *Laographia* 19:366–378.
Kurtz, Donna, and John Boardman
    1971 *Greek Burial Customs*. Ithaca, N.Y.: Cornell University Press.
Lawson, John C.
    1910 *Modern Greek Folklore and Ancient Greek Religion*. Cambridge: At the University Press.
Leach, Edmund
    1970 *Claude Lévi-Strauss*. New York: The Viking Press.
    1972 Two Essays Concerning the Symbolic Representation of Time. In *Reader in Comparative Religion*. 3d ed., ed. W. Lessa and E. Vogt, pp. 108–116. New York: Harper & Row.
    1976 *Culture and Communication*. Cambridge: At the University Press.
Lévi-Strauss, Claude
    1963 *Structural Anthropology*. New York: Basic Books.
    1966a *The Savage Mind*. Chicago: University of Chicago Press.
    1966b The Culinary Triangle. *New Society* (London) 166:937–940.
    1967 The Story of Asdiwal. In *The Structural Study of Myth and Totemism*, ed. E. Leach, pp. 1–47. London: Tavistock.
    1970 *Tristes Tropiques*. New York: Atheneum.
Lianidis, Simos
    1964 Nekrika kai taphika sti Santa tou Pontou. *Archeion Pontou* 26:159–176.
Lioudaki, Maria
    1939 I teleuti stin Kriti. *Epetiris tis Etaireias Kritikon Spoudon* 2:403–427.
Litsas, F. K.
    1976 Rousalia: The Ritual Worship of the Dead. In *The Realm of the Extra*

Human: Agents and Audiences, ed. A. Bharati, pp. 447–465. Paris: Mouton.

Loli, N.
1974 Taphika ethima kai epikideioi teletai. *Ipeirotiki Estia* 23:640–647.

Lord, Albert
1971 *The Singer of Tales*. New York: Atheneum.

Loukatos, Dimitris
1940 Laographikai peri teleutis endeixeis para Ioanni Chrysostomo. *Epetiris tou Laographikou Archeiou* 2:30–117.
1977 *Eisagogi stin elliniki laographia*. Athens: Morphotiko Idryma Ethnikis Trapezis.

Malinowski, Bronislaw
1954 *Magic, Science and Religion*. Garden City, N.Y.: Doubleday Anchor Books.

Mastrantonis, George
nd[a] *Death, The Threshold to Eternal Life*. St. Louis: Orthodox Lore of the Gospel of Our Savior.
nd[b] *Traditions, Symbols and Customs: Their Proper Use and Abuse*. St. Louis: Orthodox Lore of the Gospel of Our Savior.

Megas, George
1940 Zitimata ellinikis laographias: Ta kata tin teleutin. *Epetiris tou Laographikou Archeiou* 2:166–205.
1963 *Greek Calendar Customs*. Athens.

Mousaiou-Bouyioukou, K.
1965 I thani kai o thrinos sto Livisi kai ti Makri tis Lykias. *Mikrasiatika Chronika* 12:53–78.

Muşlea, Jean
1925 La mort-mariage: une particularité du folklore balcanique. *Mélanges de l'école roumaine en France* 3–32.

Passow, Arnoldus
1972 *Popularia carmina Graeciae recentioris*. Athens: Tegopoulos-Nikas. (1st ed. 1860.)

Pazinis, Goustavos
nd *O alanthastos oneirokritis*. New York: Atlantis.

Petropoulos, Dimitris
    1959   *Ellinika dimotika tragoudia.* Vol. 2. Athens: Zacharopoulos.
Politis, N. G.
    1978   *Eklogai apo ta tragoudia tou ellinikou laou.* Athens: Vayionakis.
Prevelakis, Pantelis
    1976   *To chroniko mias politeias.* Athens: Estia. (*Tale of a Town.* Trans. K.
            Johnstone. London-Athens: Doric Publications, 1976.)
Rabinow, Paul
    1977   *Reflections on Fieldwork in Morocco.* Berkeley: University of Cali-
            fornia Press.
Radcliffe-Brown, A. R.
    1933   *The Andaman Islanders.* Cambridge: At the University Press.
Rosaldo, Michelle, and Louise Lamphere, ed.
    1974   *Woman, Culture, and Society.* Stanford, Calif.: Stanford University
            Press.
Rush, Alfred
    1941   *Death and Burial in Christian Antiquity.* Washington, D.C.: Catholic
            University of America Press.
Schwimmer, Eric
    1980   Review of *The Role of the Reader: Explorations in the Semiotics of
            Texts,* by U. Eco. *American Anthropologist* 82:867–868.
Seferis, George
    1967   *George Seferis: Collected Poems 1924–1955.* Trans. and ed. E. Keeley
            and P. Sherrard. Princeton, N.J.: Princeton University Press.
Stamouli-Saranti, E.
    1929   Apo ta ethima tis Thrakis. *Thrakika* 2:131–151.
Synkollitis, S.
    1934   O nekros eis tin Anaselitsa. *Laographia* 11:387–414.
Tuffin, Paul
    1972   The Whitening Crow: Some *Adynata* in the Greek Tradition. *Epetiris
            tou Kentrou Epistimonikon Ereunon* (Lefkosia, Cyprus) 6:79–92.
Turner, Victor
    1967   *The Forest of Symbols.* Ithaca, N.Y.: Cornell University Press.

Tylor, Edward B.
  1920   *Primitive Culture.* New York: G. P. Putnam's Sons. (1st ed. 1871.)
Van Gennep, Arnold
  1960   *The Rites of Passage.* Chicago: University of Chicago Press. (1st French ed. 1909.)
Vaporis, N. M.
  1977   *An Orthodox Prayer Book.* Brookline, Mass.: Holy Cross Orthodox Press.
Vermeule, Emily
  1979   *Aspects of Death in Early Greek Art and Poetry.* Berkeley: University of California Press.
Wallace, A.F.C.
  1959   The Institutionalization of Cathartic and Control Strategies in Iroquois Religious Psychotherapy. In *Culture and Mental Health*, ed. M. K. Opler. New York: MacMillan.
Ware, Timothy
  1963   *The Orthodox Church.* Harmondsworth, Middlesex: Penguin Books.
Young, Allen
  1975   Why Amhara Get Kureynya: Sickness and Possession in an Ethiopian Zar Cult. *American Ethnologist* 2:567–584.
Zafeirakopoulos, D. K.
  1911   Ethima tis kideias en Mani. *Laographia* 3:473–477.

INDEX

Numbers in italic type refer to the photographs.

INDEX

Library of Congress Cataloging in Publication Data

Danforth, Loring M., 1949-
  The death rituals of rural Greece.

  Bibliography: p.   Includes index.
  1. Funeral rites and ceremonies—Greece.   2. Greece—Rural condition.
3. Death—Social aspects—Greece.
I. Tsiaras, Alexander. II. Title.   GT3251.A2D36   1982   393'.09495
82-47589
ISBN 0-691-03132-0   AACR2   ISBN 0-691-00027-1 (pbk.)

169

PHOTOGRAPHS

PLATE 1

    Vassilis died suddenly of a heart attack early in January. He was well liked because of the stories and jokes he used to tell at the village coffeehouse. He was also well respected because he had many relatives and because he had arranged successful marriages for all five of his daughters. His death cast such a pall over Potamia that the village festival that takes place on January 18 in honor of Saint Athanasios was canceled.

    With Vassilis' body lying on a low bed in the formal reception room of his house, his wife Sotiria laments his death. She calls out to him with her hand to her mouth, as if to make sure that her voice carries over the long distance that separates them. Sotiria was widowed for the first time at the age of twenty-four, after only a few years of marriage. She had been a widow for six years before marrying Vassilis. Now she is a widow again. A short time before Vassilis' death Sotiria had a dream. She saw her mother, who had died several years earlier, enter the kitchen and light the stove. Smoke and soot filled the house, and all was black.

PLATE 2

Thanasis' death was one of the most tragic anyone could remember. He had lived and worked in the United States for seven years and was about to be married. During this time his mother had begged him repeatedly to come back to Greece to see his family. Living abroad for so long was almost like being dead. Finally Thanasis relented and returned to Greece. Upon his arrival in Athens, airport officials took him into custody, and he was inducted into the army immediately. Three months later an army truck he was driving went off the road and rolled over. Thanasis died instantly. His skull had been crushed.

When Thanasis finally returned home, when his mother finally saw him after so many years, he had been dead for several days. Some people suggested that the funeral take place right away. His mother, however, insisted that Thanasis remain in the house overnight and be buried the following day. It would be the last chance she would have to see him, the last night he would spend at home with his family.

Because Thanasis had never married, his funeral was celebrated "like a wedding." A white wedding crown was placed on his head, and wedding songs were sung over his body as funeral laments. Thanasis' funeral would be his wedding. He was about to marry the black earth.

PLATE 3

Mihalis died in his sleep sometime in the early hours of the morning. His body was washed, dressed in a new suit set aside specifically for this occasion, and laid out on a low bed that had been covered with a beautiful hand-woven sheet. His feet and hands were tied and his lower jaw bound shut with strips of white cloth. Flowers, candles, and Mihalis' favorite cap were then placed on his body. A small olive-oil lamp was lit and set by his head.

All day Mihalis' close relatives tended his body with tears and laments. By late afternoon the room was filled with more distant relatives and fellow villagers who had gathered for the funeral. When the village priest entered the room, dressed in his tall, black, cylindrical hat and his richly embroidered purple and gold robes, all crying and lamenting quickly ceased. Many people left the room.

Mihalis' closest relatives stand as the priest, holding a censer in his right hand and a lit candle and a prayer book in his left, begins to recite the *Trisayio*, a portion of the Orthodox funeral service.

> Alas! What an agony the soul endures when from the body it is parting; how many are her tears for weeping, but there is none that will show compassion: unto the angels she turns with downcast eyes; useless are her supplications; and unto men she extends her imploring hands, but finds none to bring her rescue. (Vaporis 1977:107)

PLATE 4

Because Thanasis died while serving in the army, a Greek flag lies draped over his body. Two cousins lift up his coffin in preparation for the funeral procession. They wear white handkerchiefs in their breast pockets to mark their status as *bratimia*, "men of honor" who assist in the performance of marriage rites.

Thanasis is now about to depart on his long journey to the church, to the grave, to the world of the dead. He is leaving his home for the last time. This moment is a particularly powerful one. It is an important point in the separation of the deceased from his relatives. The grieving of the mourners reaches a climax. Thanasis' bereaved relatives cry out with open mouths, as if to delay somehow his imminent departure.

—Τίνος εἶν' τὸ ἄλογο
ποὺ στέκει ἔξω στὴν αὐλή;
—Τοῦ Θανάση μ' εἶναι τ' ἄλογο
ποὺ στέκει ἔξω στὴν αὐλή.
Ὅλοι τρογύρω ἐλᾶτε,
νὰ τὸν ξεπροβοδίσουμε.
Θὰ ξενητευτῆ πολὺ μακριά,
καὶ πίσω δὲ γυρίζει.

"Whose horse is that
standing out in the yard?"
"It is Thanasis' horse
that is standing out in the yard.
Everyone gather round,
so that we may send him off together.
He will go far away to a distant land,
and he will never return.

PLATE 5

The funeral procession moves slowly and somberly through the village streets. Three women dressed in black carry the food that will be distributed after the burial—a tray of boiled wheat known as *koliva* and a basket of bread, pastries, and candy. One woman carries a pitcher of wine to be poured over the body of the deceased before he is covered with earth. Behind these women the black rectangle of the coffin lid is visible above the bowed heads of those who accompany the deceased on his final journey from his home to the village church.

Three young boys, serving as acolytes, carry a cross and two staffs crowned with metal representations of six-winged cherubim. They are followed by the three priests who have been invited to perform the funeral service at this particularly tragic death. Behind them are the coffin and the close relatives of the deceased.

> Καλὰ τ' ἀποχαιρέτηξε, παιδί μου, τὰ σοκάκια,
> γιατὶ δὲν τὰ ξαναπερνοῦν τ' ἄσπρα σου ποδαράκια.
> (Lioudaki 1939:417)

> My child, bid farewell to these narrow streets,
> for your white little feet will never walk them again.

PLATE 6

Thodora's death came as a relief to her children. She was very old and senile, and had been unable to care for herself for several years. When she died on Easter Sunday it was as if people were hurrying to be done with her funeral so they could resume the Easter festivities that had been temporarily interrupted by her death.

Here Thodora lies in a plain wooden coffin in the center of the village church. On her body lie coins and flowers placed there earlier by her friends and relatives. At her waist is an icon of the Resurrection of Christ. The small group of mourners stands in a close circle around her body, holding lighted candles as the village priest recites the funeral service:

> Brethren, we would not have you ignorant concerning those who are asleep, that you may not grieve as others do who have no hope. For since we believe that Jesus died and rose again, even so, through Jesus, God will bring with him those who have fallen asleep. . . . For the Lord himself will descend from heaven with a cry of command, with the archangel's call, and with the sound of the trumpet of God. And the dead in Christ will rise first; then we who are alive, who are left, shall be caught up together with them in the clouds to meet the Lord in the air, and we shall always be with the Lord.
>
> (Vaporis 1977:110)

PLATE 7

During the funeral service Thanasis' two brothers stood at the head of the coffin. Here one brother, overcome with emotion, collapses into the arms of those standing behind him. When relatives and fellow villagers gathered at his house before the funeral, Thanasis' brother told them not to show any sympathy toward his mother. He blamed her for his brother's death. If she had not pressured him to return to Greece, he would still be alive. His family would now be celebrating his wedding instead of his funeral.

Throughout the church service Thanasis' brother remained at the edge of consciousness. At the end of the service he collapsed again and was carried out of the church unconscious shortly after the coffin bearing the dead body of his brother was carried out and taken to the graveyard.

PLATE 8

Brethren, come, and let us a farewell kiss give to him whom death has taken, and offer thanks to God. For he has departed from the bosom of his kin; and he hastens to burial, no longer remembering vanity, nor yet the flesh which is often sore distressed. Where are now his kindred and comrades? Now is come the hour of partings: let us pray to the Lord to bring him to his rest. (Vaporis 1977:116)

At the conclusion of the funeral service all those who have gathered in the church file past the open coffin, place some coins on Thanasis' body, and kiss both the icon lying there and his forehead. This is another powerful moment in the departure of the deceased from his family and the world of the living. Thanasis' young niece, standing to the right of his body, seems almost untouched by the power and the tragedy of the death that has taken place.

Ὅλα σου τὰ φιλήματα γλυκά ἤτανε σὰ μέλι,
μὰ τὸ στερνό σου φίλημα, πικρό εἶναι σὰ φαρμάκι.
Πικρό ἤτανε καὶ τὸ φίλημα, πικρὸς κι ὁ χωρισμός σου,
ἔσκυψα νὰ σ' ἀνασπαστῶ καὶ πῆρα τὸν καημό σου.
(Petropoulos 1959:221)

All the kisses I have given you were as sweet as honey,
but the last kiss I gave you was as bitter as poison.
The kiss was bitter and so was your departure.
I bent over to kiss you and I tasted the grief on your lips.

PLATE 9

At the conclusion of the funeral service, after her relatives and friends have greeted her with a kiss for the last time, Thodora is carried out of the cool, musty darkness of the village church into the bright light of the Easter day on which she died. The rituals of funeral and burial involve many such transitions from dark to light and from light to dark. Only a short time ago, in another painful departure, Thodora was taken from the reception room of her house—lit only by candles and filled with the smell of wax, incense, perfume, and death—into the sunny village streets for the funeral procession to the church. In a few moments she will leave the light of day and the world of the living for the final time to enter the dark, damp earth and the shadowy world of the dead.

> Σήμερα ἐγίνη ἀλαλαγμός,
> ὁ ἥλιος ἐσκοτείνιασε. . . .
> Σήμερα ἐγίνηκε σεισμός. . . .
> Σκοτάδι χειμωνιάτικο
> κι ἡμέρα νύχτα ἔγινε.
>   (Alexiou 1974:168)

> Today there has been a great cry,
> the sun has darkened. . . .
> Today there has been an earthquake. . . .
> There is winter blackness,
> and day has turned into night.
>   (Alexiou)

PLATE 10

Mihalis' body lies in a coffin in the village graveyard. Behind him in a row stand his close female relatives. The two women on the right cross themselves as the priest recites prayers from the funeral service in memory of the deceased.

> Looking on me as I lie here prone before you, voiceless and un-
> breathing, mourn for me, everyone—brethren and friends, kindred,
> and you who knew me well; for but yesterday with you I was talking,
> and suddenly there came upon me the fearful hour of death.
> (Vaporis 1977:117)

At the edge of the graveyard, tall and dark as if in mourning themselves, stand two cypress trees.

> Κυπαρίσσ' εἶχα στὸ σπίτι,
> κυπαρίσσι στὸν ὀντά μου.
> Φύσηξε βοριᾶς κι ἀέρας.
> Γκρέμισε τὸ κυπαρίσσι,
> κι ἔχασα τὸ στήριγμά μου.

> I had a cypress tree in my house.
> I had a cypress tree in my room.
> The north wind blew.
> It toppled the cypress tree,
> and I lost my pillar of strength.

PLATE 11

Above, the intricate patterns of the priests' gold and purple vestments and the richly decorated gold censer contrast sharply with the simple black clothes of the bereaved villagers. At the feet of his relatives lies Mihalis, his cap on his head, ready to be lowered into the freshly dug grave that gapes ominously beside him.

Ἄχ! Ἀδερφάκι μου καλό, καὶ πῶς θὰ μπῆς στὸν Ἅδη,
ἀπού 'ναι μαῦρος, σκοτεινός, βαθὺς σὰν τὸ πηγάδι;
(Lioudaki 1939:419)

Ah, my dear brother, how will you descend into Hades?
It is black, dark, and deep as a well.

PLATE 12

The village priest pours red wine in the pattern of a cross over the body of Thanasis as it lies in a coffin deep in the grave. At this time he recites a portion of the funeral service in which the deceased appears to call out to the living:

> You shall sprinkle me with hyssop and I shall be clean. You shall wash me and I shall be whiter than snow. (Vaporis 1977:118)

Whiteness here refers metaphorically to the purity of the soul of the deceased, which, it is hoped, will be cleansed of its sins and come to rest in paradise. It refers literally to the whiteness of the bones of the deceased, which will be exhumed five years hence.

At the very edge of the grave Thanasis' young niece gazes down intently into the open grave below. To the left stands the wooden coffin lid, which will close down over Thanasis all too soon.

> Σύρε, μάνα μ', γιὰ ψωμί, ψωμὶ νὰ φᾶμε βράδυ.
> Πάρε κι ἕνα παλιὸ κρασὶ 'πὸ τὸ μέγα μοναστήρι,
> νὰ πλένω τὰ λαβώματα ποὺ εἶμαι λαβωμένος.
> Πικρό, μάνα μ', τὸ λάβωμα, φαρμάκι τὸ μολύβι.

> Mother, go get some bread for us to eat tonight,
> and get some fine old wine from the great monastery,
> so that I can wash the wounds I have suffered.
> Mother, my wound is deep and the bullet's poison is bitter.

PLATE 13

Like a blossom that wastes away, and like a dream that passes
and is gone, so is every mortal into dust resolved. . . .
The earth is the Lord's, and the fullness thereof; the world, and
all that dwell therein. You are dust, and to dust you will return.

(Vaporis 1977:107 and 118)

After pouring wine over Thodora's body the village priest, followed by
everyone present at the grave, tosses a small amount of earth over the body.
This gesture indicates that all the members of the community of the living
have fulfilled their obligation to provide the deceased with a proper burial.

According to one report (Lioudaki 1939:406), in Crete the following phrase
is traditionally uttered shortly after a person's death: "This very earth which
nourished you will eat you as well." This phrase expresses the desire that the
corpse decompose completely to ensure proper separation of the deceased from
the world of the living and final incorporation into the world of the dead.

Καὶ πῶς θὰ τὸ καλοδεχτῆς νὰ κατεβῆς στὸν Ἅδη,
νὰ βάλης σκέπασμα τὴ γῆ, τὴν πέτρα μαξελάρι;

(Lioudaki 1939:419)

How will you bear going down into Hades,
covering yourself with a blanket of earth, and resting your head on a
pillow of rock?

PLATE 14

The caretaker of the village church has climbed down into the grave in order to draw the shroud up over Thanasis' face before placing the cover on the coffin.

For many hours now the attention of all those present, both mourners and photographer alike, has been focused exclusively on the body of the deceased. When the village priest finished reciting the *Trisayio*, he suddenly turned to the photographer, Alexander Tsiaras, and asked him if he wanted to take any more photographs. Until that moment the priest had never spoken to Tsiaras; until that day he had never even seen him. Tsiaras, the outsider, had suddenly taken the place of the deceased as the center of attention. The line between participant and observer had been crossed. The frame of the ritual drama had been broken as the photographer stepped on stage and assumed a role himself.

PLATE 15

For consigned to the grave is he; with stone is he to be covered.
Darkness is his dwelling place; he with the dead is entombed. Come,
all you his kindred and comrades: now is come the hour of parting.
Let us pray to the Lord to bring him to his rest. (Vaporis 1977:116)

The lid has been placed on Thanasis' coffin. Now that visual contact with
the body of the deceased has been cut off, the emotional intensity of the
moment dies down. People turn away from the grave as the first shovelfuls of
earth begin to cover the coffin.

> Κι ἂν κλαῖτε κι ἂν θλιβόσαστε, κάλλιο εἴσαστ' ἀπὸ μένα.
> Ἐσεῖς δειπνᾶτε μὲ τὸ φῶς, κοιμᾶστε στὰ στρωμένα,
> μὰ 'γὼ εἶμαι στὰ σκοτεινά, στὰ κρυοπαγωμένα,
> χωρὶς παχιὰ παπλώματα, δίχως παχιὰ στρωσίδια.
> (Petropoulos 1959:239)

Even if you are crying, even if you are grieving, remember: you are
    better off than I.
You dine by daylight and sleep in comfortable beds,
while I lie in the dark and in the freezing cold,
without heavy blankets, without thick mattresses.

PLATE 16

Today no more tears will be shed; no more laments will be sung. Mihalis' relatives and friends have returned to his house for the traditional funeral meal. In the now empty graveyard several village men fill in Mihalis' grave. Their relaxed and casual attitude contrasts markedly with the intense emotion that so recently filled the graveyard.

In the foreground is a rather dilapidated cage-like enclosure, made of wood, which marks the grave of an old and almost forgotten villager. Perched at the head of this grave is a small box where a photograph and an olive-oil lamp are kept. Behind Mihalis' grave stands the village ossuary, which will receive Mihalis' bones when he is exhumed five years hence.

Ὁ ἀποθαμένος δὲ μιλεῖ, γιατὶ δὲν ἔχει στόμα,
γιατὶ τόνε σκεπάζουνε μὲ πέτρες καὶ μὲ χῶμα.
(Lioudaki 1939:410)

The dead man does not speak, because he has no mouth,
and because they are covering him with rocks and with earth.

PLATE 17

The sound of church bells ringing slowly in mourning calls the women of Potamia to one of the long series of memorial services performed during the five-year period following death.

Young children have gathered in the courtyard, which lies between the village church and the graveyard, to play near the memorial to the men of Potamia who died in battle. Inside the graveyard, even after women have begun to lament, the voices of children at play can still be heard. They play until the memorial service is over and their mothers return from the graveyard to the church courtyard, from the world of the dead to the world of the living. Then they can enjoy the bread, pastries, candy, and *koliva* that will be distributed at the conclusion of the memorial service.

The black dress of the four women in mourning, starkly outlined here against the gray cement of the church courtyard, dramatizes the blackness of everything associated with death. Haros, the huntsman, who makes off with the souls of the dead when the hour of death is at hand, "is black, is dressed in black, and rides a black horse" (Politis 1978:227).

PLATE 18

Three days after Vassilis' death his grave is still nothing more than a simple mound of fresh earth. The memorial service performed at this time is the first occasion on which his relatives visit his grave. The three-day period following death is associated with the three days Christ lay in his tomb prior to his resurrection from the dead on Easter.

Vassilis' wife Sotiria, standing at the foot of the grave, is accompanied by her daughters and her husband's sisters. She holds out her arms toward Vassilis' grave, overcome with emotion at seeing for the first time what will be Vassilis' home, her second home, for the next five years. The women carry large white candles, which they will light and place on the grave.

Some time after her husband's death Sotiria dreamed that he returned home late at night. The house was dark. She said to him, "Vassilis, turn on the light." He replied: "You are in the dark now. You have no light."

PLATE 19

Vassilis' daughters light their candles and place them on the earth mound above their father's three-day-old grave. Then they sit down with their handkerchiefs in their hands and begin to cry and sing.

Τί νὰ σοῦ στείλω, ξένε μου, τί νὰ σοῦ προβοδίσω; . . .
Νὰ στείλω μὲ τὰ δάκρυα μου μαντήλι μουσκεμένο,
τὰ δάκρυα μού εἶναι καυτερά, καὶ καῖνε τὸ μαντήλι.
Τί νὰ σοῦ στείλω, ξένε μου, τί νὰ σοῦ προβοδίσω;
(Politis 1978:199–200)

What can I send you, stranger? What can I give you as you depart? . . .
With my tears I will send you a damp handkerchief.
My tears were burning hot, and they burned the handkerchief.
What can I send you, stranger? What can I give you as your depart?

Sotiria once compared a human life to a candle. As long as the candle burns, the person remains alive; but when the flame goes out the soul departs, and the person dies. Sotiria, her daughters, and her husband's sisters sit and cry and sing for almost an hour, as the candles burn down slowly, growing shorter and shorter, until the flames flicker and die.

PLATE 20

Those who can afford it build very elaborate and very expensive marble monuments to honor the memory of their dead relatives. In the center of these graves is an open area covered with gravel where flowers are planted and candles are set. At the head of the most elaborate graves stands a marble-and-glass case where an oil lamp and a photograph of the deceased are kept.

These monuments must be built before the performance of the memorial service that is celebrated forty days after death. The soul of the deceased is said to linger on earth for forty days, at which time it ascends to heaven to be judged by God, just as Christ ascended to heaven on the fortieth day after his resurrection.

Sotiria sits at the head of the grave holding her handkerchief to her cheek. Many of the women lining both sides of the grave gaze down at Vassilis' photograph as they sing and weep for him. Directly behind Vassilis' grave a widow tends the grave of her husband. Soon she will join the other women at Vassilis' grave, adding her voice to theirs, as they lament together the deaths that have touched them all.

PLATE 21

When Father Andrew arrives at Vassilis' grave, the singing of laments quickly stops. With only an occasional sob to disturb the sudden quiet that has fallen over the graveyard, the bereaved women stand up and light small candles that have been hurriedly passed around. As Father Andrew incenses over the grave, the smell of frankincense and the sound of the small bells on the censer fill the air. He begins to recite the *Trisayio*:

> Blessed is our God always, both now and ever, and to the ages of ages. Amen. Holy God, Holy Mighty, Holy Immortal, have mercy on us. Glory to the Father and to the Son and to the Holy Spirit, now and ever, and to the ages of ages. Amen. (Vaporis 1977:98)

Sotiria stands to the left of Father Andrew. In front of her is her granddaughter Sotiroula, who, Sotiria once said, will cry for her when she dies. Peering curiously over the gray cinder-block wall that separates the graveyard from the church courtyard are three young children. Their presence, marginal and distant as it is, suggests the ambivalent feelings of their parents concerning their attendance at rituals associated with death. Children too must encounter death, but preferably from a safe distance.

PLATE 22

When the village priest has finished reciting the *Trisayio* at funerals, memorial services, and exhumations, people gather in the church courtyard for the distribution of food. Here women hand out bread and pastries from large wicker baskets. They spoon out *koliva* decorated with sugar, raisins, nuts, and spices from large metal pans. They also distribute cognac, candy, and other sweets in memory of the dead.

Everyone who receives a portion of food responds with a wish that God may forgive the deceased. People say that this food is distributed "so that the dead may eat." The food consumed by the living is believed to pass over somehow into the other world where it becomes available to the souls of the dead.

Several days after a memorial service performed in memory of her husband, a widow saw a dream in which her dead husband appeared to her and said: "Why do you just bring me *koliva*? You know I never liked it. Why don't you ever bring me any rice pudding?" The following Saturday she baked some bread and made some rice pudding. That evening she brought them to the graveyard and distributed them to the women who had gathered there. She never saw her husband in her sleep again. That was a good sign, she said. It meant that her husband was happy, satisfied, and well fed.

PLATE 23

Anna, like many other women, often attends death rituals performed for people to whom she is not related. That is the reason she is not dressed completely in black here. Anna is shouting angrily at her young son, who has just run off with his hands full of pastries, hard candy, and Turkish delight. She is upset because he has left the church courtyard without washing his hands at the faucet by the gate. All who attend death rituals have come in contact with death and must therefore wash in order to cleanse themselves of its taint.

The woman to the left of Anna is bringing home as much food as she can carry. Some men will not eat this food. They say it is food for the dead, not for the living.

PLATE 24

Several miles from Potamia lies the village of Kerasovo. The cemetery of Kerasovo is located on the crest of a hill about fifteen minutes by foot from the edge of the village. It is much larger than the cemetery of Potamia and is overgrown with bushes, weeds, and lush green grass. The graves of some of the poorer villagers lie at the back of the graveyard and are not well cared for. The only way to identify one of these graves is by the faded photograph kept in the small metal box at the head of the grave.

Early one Sunday shortly after Easter, while most village women are in church, Matinio, the widow who performs most of the exhumations in Kerasovo, begins to open the grave of an old man who is now about to leave his cold dark home beneath the earth and return to the upper world, the world of the living, from which he departed poor and alone five years earlier.

> Μαστόροι ποὺ δουλεύετε στὸ σπίτι τὸ δικό μου,
> ἀπὸ τὴ δέξια τὴ μεριὰ ν' ἀφῆστε παραθύρι,
> νὰ μπαῖν', νὰ βγαῖνε τὰ πουλιά, τῆς ἄνοιξης τ' ἀδόνια,
> νὰ ἰδῶ πότ' ἔρθεται ἡ ἄνοιξη, πότε τὸ καλοκαίρι,
> νὰ 'ρχωνται τὰ παιδάκια μου, γλυκὰ νὰ κουβεντιάζω.
> Τίποτας δὲ φοβήθηκα μέσ' στὸν Ἀπάνω κόσμο
> καὶ τούτ' τὴν ὥρα σήμερα ἔχω μεγάλο φόβο.
> Ἀκούω τὰ φκιάρια ποὺ βροντοῦν καὶ τὰ τσαπιὰ ποὺ σκάβουν.
>
> (Kosmas 1960:373)

You who are working on my house,
put a window on the right side
for the birds, the nightingales of spring, to come and go,
so that I can see when spring and summer arrive,
so that my children can come and talk with me sweetly.
I never feared anything at all in the upper world,
but now, today, I am very much afraid.
I hear the shovels' thunder; I hear the hoes' sharp ring.

PLATE 25

Where is now our gold, and our silver? Where is now the surging crowd of domestics, and their busy cries? All is dust, all is ashes, all is shadow. . . .

I called to mind the Prophet who shouted, "I am but earth and ash." And once again I looked with understanding on the tombs, and I saw the bones therein which of flesh were naked; and I said, "Which indeed is he that is king? Or which is soldier? Which is the wealthy, which the needy? Which the righteous, or which the sinner?" (Vaporis 1977:108)

PLATE 26

Kostas had made many enemies in his life. People said that during the Civil War he had killed a man. That was why his death had been such a long and painful one. He talked deliriously about the sins he had committed and the people he had wronged. His soul would not leave his body. Finally Kostas' family brought a priest to hear his confession. Shortly thereafter Kostas died.

Many people believe that if someone has committed many sins, or if his sins have not been forgiven, then his body will not decompose, and his bones will be covered with flesh and hair when they are exhumed. For this reason Kostas' family decided not to exhume his remains five years after his death, as is customary, but to wait two additional years. During this time Kostas' daughter, who was known throughout the village as a very religious person, frequently invited the local priest to read prayers and perform liturgies in behalf of her father's soul.

When Kostas' remains were finally exhumed seven years after his death, a large group of women gathered at his grave, waiting with thinly veiled curiosity to see if the condition of his bones would confirm the judgment they had made on his character while he was still alive.

Gazing down from the graveyard wall, village children watch the exhumation from a proper distance. Past the wide, rocky bed of the Titarisios stand rows of poplar trees that bound the village fields beyond.

PLATE 27

Kostas' bones are being piled at the edge of his grave between some candles and the pitcher of wine in which his bones will soon be washed. One woman leans over the open grave and points to some of the many small bones of the hands. She wants to make sure that no bones are left behind in the mud and forgotten.

Kostas' remains were not placed in the village ossuary together with the remains of all the other villagers. They were immediately reburied in the same grave from which they had come. This was done because his relatives were afraid that a descendant of the man Kostas had murdered might take his bones from the ossuary and burn them.

Six months later the wife of Kostas' brother died. She was buried in this same grave on top of the box containing Kostas' remains. A short time later Kostas' wife had a dream in which Kostas appeared to her and said: "It's crowded down here. Take me out." But it was too late. Nothing could be done. Kostas' bones now lay beneath the body of his brother's wife.

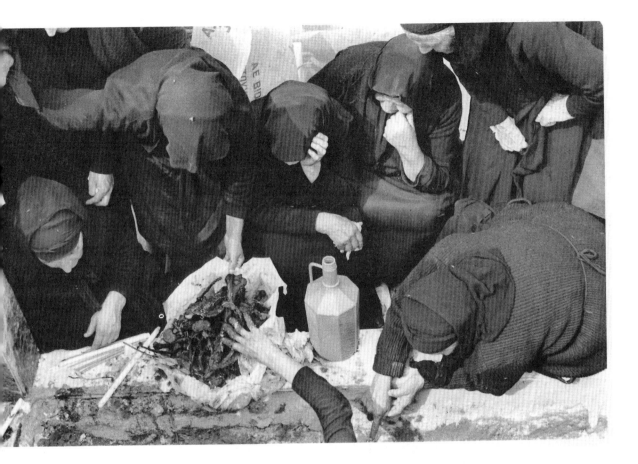

PLATE 28

Matinio has reached the point where the earth in the grave suddenly becomes darker and pieces of rotten wood begin to appear. She has laid aside her hoe, put on rubber gloves, and begun to dig with her hands. Some of the women who have gathered around the grave sob quietly, drying their tears frequently with their handkerchiefs. Others peer into the grave to check on Matinio's progress and note the condition of the bones as they are removed from the grave. Slowly the jumbled pile of bones on the large white kerchief grows larger. The deceased rises bone by bone from the grave.

> Truly, truly, I say to you, the hour is coming, and now is when the dead will hear the voice of the Son of God, and those who hear will live. . . . Do not marvel at this; for the hour is coming when all who are in the tombs will hear his voice and come forth, those who have done good, to the resurrection of life, and those who have done evil to the resurrection of judgment. (Vaporis 1977:111)

Women often say that exhumations are performed so that the dead may see the light of day for the last time, so that a heavy weight may be removed from their chests. Some women even say that just before an exhumation they feel a sense of eagerness and excitement. They think they are about to see the deceased again—alive.

> Γιὰ σήκω, κόρη, ἀπὸ τὴν γῆν, γιὰ σήκω ἀπὸ τὸ χῶμα,
> γιὰ νὰ ἰδῆς τὴ μανούλα σου, ποὺ σὲ προσμένει ἀκόμα.
> (Petropoulos 1959:233)

Get up, young woman! Rise up from the earth,
so that you can see your mother who is waiting for you still.

PLATE 29

When the women who have gathered around the grave confront a pile of bones instead of the person they buried five years earlier, their hopes are crushed. The joy they anticipated is transformed into grief and pain. They are forced to realize that although the exhumation can return the remains of the deceased to the upper world, it cannot reverse the process of decomposition, which has reduced a person to bones. It cannot bring the dead back to life.

Ἰβώ ’βαλα στὴ μαύρη γῆν τριαντάφυλλα κι ρόδα,
κι τώρα ἦρτα κι ἔβγαλα κυδώνια σαπιμένα.
(Mousaiou-Bouyioukou 1965:71)

I placed roses in the black earth.
Just now I came and took out rotten quinces.

When all the bones have been removed from the grave, everyone grows quiet. Then comments are made about the fragility of human life and the futility of human strivings: "That's what we should look at. That's all he is— a pile of bones. Where is all his money? Where are all his troubles, all his worries?" At this moment everyone present at the exhumation is confronted with tangible evidence of human mortality and of the ultimate fate that awaits us all.

PLATE 30

Matinio has just lifted the skull from the grave and turned abruptly toward Alexander Tsiaras. She asked him if he wanted to photograph her holding the skull in her hands. As Tsiaras photographed Matinio, she addressed him directly: "We'll all look like this in the end. Some day you'll see the remains of your mother and father exhumed this way. Some day you'll be exhumed, then you'll look like this too."

With these words Matinio incorporated Tsiaras forcefully into her reality, into the world of death as she experienced it. Photographer and subject, observer and participant, had been united before the grim face of death.

PLATE 31

When the skull is lifted from the earth, the woman performing the exhumation wraps it in a white kerchief and crosses herself. Then she greets the deceased with a kiss and welcomes him to the world of the living. Next she hands the skull to a close relative of the deceased, saying, "You have received him well," the phrase addressed to those who have recently welcomed relatives returning home from a long journey. The skull is then passed from hand to hand, as relatives and fellow village women greet it in turn. When all the bones have been removed from the grave, the village priest arrives to recite the *Trisayio* and wash them in wine. At this point the material remains of the deceased have reached final and permanent form and are placed in the village ossuary, the collective home of the village dead, where they will rest for eternity.